Essential Psychology

for
Modern Organizations

also by Patrick Heller

Booklet

Agile Essentials for Modern Leadership

Essential Psychology

for
Modern Organizations

Practical scientifically proven psychological insights
into your mind and everyday interactions
with colleagues at work

Patrick Heller

ISBN-13: 979-8-6766-3943-3

Keywords: 1. Psychology, 2. Organization, 3. Work.

Cover design & photography: Petra de Krom

All other artwork: Patrick Heller

To Petra, Kian & Reno,

for all your love, patience and support

The use of the singular "they"

In writing this book, I've used the singular "they" throughout the book to actively apply a gender-neutral policy. It might take some getting used to when reading, but I must say, in writing it's easy to get used to – and it beats the silly phrasing "he/she" or "he or she". So, instead of "when an employee comes in, he or she walks straight to the coffee machine first thing in the morning", it now is, "when an employee comes in, they walk straight to the coffee machine first thing in the morning".

I didn't apply this policy to appease a politically correct audience, but more from a psychological perspective. We'll see in this book that we are all prone to fall victim to biases, prejudice, and stereotypes – no matter how neutral we think we are. The only way to deal with these biases is to *actively* circumvent them.

Patrick Heller.

After everything is doubted,

stand for what is left standing

Brief Contents

Preface — *Who should read this book and why?*

Introduction — *Your personal use of the book*

Chapter One — Beware the Nonsense
Chapter Two — The Self
Chapter Three — The Self and Others
Chapter Four — Therapy as Coaching
Chapter Five — What's Next?
Chapter Six — The History of Psychology
Chapter Seven — The History of Work

Epilogue — Proceed with Caution

Appendix A — *Timelines of Psychology, Work & History*

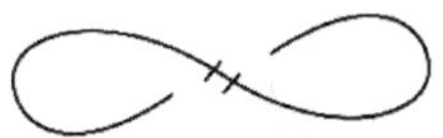

Contents

The use of the singular "they" vii

Brief Contents xi

Contents xiii

Preface – Who Should Read This Book and Why? 1

Someone Like Me 1

A Psychologist 3

Science in the Modern Workplace 3

This Book 4

Introduction – Your Personal Use of the Book 5

Cover to Cover 5

Short Summary 5

Changing the Order 6

Reference Book 6

Multiple Books in One 7

Awareness 7

Chapter One – Beware the Nonsense 9

I Coach People 9

Sucking It All Up 11

The Dunning-Kruger Effect 12

Fake News 14

Science is *Not* Just Another Opinion 15

No Harm, No Foul… Right? 17

Popular Myths 19

We only use 10% of our brainpower 19

There are left-brain and right-brain people 20

The female brain differs significantly from the male brain 24

We have a lizard brain inside our modern brain 28

The exciting field of neuroscience is the key to all psychological answers 31

Mirror neurons give us empathy and humanity 35

Brain-training will make you smart 37

10,000 hours of training will make you an expert in any field 40

People learn better through their preferred learning style 42

With a growth mindset, we are able to reach unknown heights 45

Personality tests are a reliable tool for hiring, firing, and setting up teams 50

DISC 52

NLP is super powerful stuff 55

Thinking yourself out of a depression 65

Toxic positivity 67

Endnote on the myths 68

Chapter Two – The Self 69

The Astonishing Hypothesis 69

The Mind and Free Will 70

Personality 71

Traits 72

OCEAN – The Big Five 73

Intelligence...74

IQ tests 75

Intelligence as a Good Predictor 77

Heritability 80

Memory...83

Learning 88

Slow and Fast Thinking...................................90

Consciousness 91

Reasoning...93

Analogies 93

Inductive Reasoning 96

The Availability Bias......................................98

The Confirmation Bias 99

The Predictable-World Bias................................102

Deduction...104

Concrete Deductive Reasoning 105

Insight Problems..106

Chapter Three – The Self and Others.....................109

The Basics of Social Psychology 109

Theory of Mind 110

Attributions 112

    Fundamental attribution error 113

Beautiful People 114

Internet Connection 115

The Pygmalion Effect 117

The Hawthorne Experiments 119

Self-esteem 121

Reference Groups 122

Self-serving Attributional Bias 125

Attitudes 127

Cognitive Dissonance 129

In-groups and Out-groups 131

Stereotypes & Prejudice 132

Social Pressure 136

    Social facilitation and social interference 136

    Choking under pressure 138

    Stereotype threat 140

Impression Management 141

Influence by Example 142

Conformity 143

Theory X & Y 147

Obedience 148

Autonomy, Mastery, and Purpose 153

Social Norms 154

The Bystander Effect 156

The Prisoner's Dilemma 162

    Tit-for-tat 164

The Ultimatum Game 165

Loss Aversion 168

Chapter Four – Therapy as Coaching 175

Team Coaching 175

    Tuckman 176

    Belbin 178

The Coach as a Therapist 181

    Psychodynamic psychotherapy 182

    Humanistic psychotherapy 183

Cognitive Behavioral Therapy 185

Behavior Therapy 186

    Contingency management 186

    Exposure treatment 187

    ABC theory of emotions 188

    Socratic questioning 192

Does Therapy Work? 195

Positive Psychology 196

Sport Psychology 198

Chapter Five – What's Next? 201

Morality 201
      Artificial Intelligence 205
      The Trolley Problem and Self-driving cars 207
Empathy 210
      Against Empathy 211
WEIRD and Beyond..215
Chapter Six – The History of Psychology.................219
A definition of psychology 219
The first modern psychologist 220
Matter over mind...221
Empiric agility...222
The Theory of Evolution 223
Freud..224
Behaviorism 227
Self-actualization...232
The cognitive revolution...234
Psychology these days..235
Chapter Seven – The History of Work.....................237
Understanding the Why 237
East India Companies...238
Industrial Revolutions 240
Scientific management 242
Project Management...249

Change Management 251

Technical background 259

Agile 263

    Manifesto for Agile Software Development 263

Epilogue – Proceed with Caution 269

The Peak of Mount Stupid 269

Where to Start after this Book 270

Appendix A – Timelines of Psychology, Work &
History 273

Timelines 273

    Psychology timeline 273

    Work timeline 275

    Timeline of major political, technical, and otherwise
    interesting events..278

Some Things to Notice 281

References...283

Index 289

About the author 300

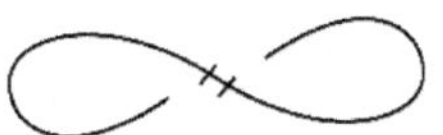

Preface – Who Should Read This Book and Why?

Of course, anyone can read this book if they like, but with whom in mind was it written and why should they care?

Someone Like Me

On the one hand, the intended audience is pretty much someone like me, somebody who works as a professional in modern organizations and has contemplated on a regular basis how useful it would be to be able to understand the human mind better. Have you often wondered *why* your colleagues do the things they do? And why in such a manner? Why do they respond to your boss' casual comments as if they were orders and completely ignore your well-founded pleas for change? If you're looking for answers to questions like these and more, then this book will surely be of interest to you.

Furthermore, if you're skeptical about the many *clickbait* wonder solutions to issues of the mind you will find in social media these days, then – by all means

– stick with this story. As I will describe in the first chapter, there is a huge difference between much of the information you find on social media and what is actually scientifically grounded. If you are – as I am – serious about your profession and indeed about not wasting your valuable time, efforts, and therefore money, you are well-advised to stick with *science.*

Why then read this book and not one of the numerous other publications about psychology? Or why not read a book about "work in the twenty-first century"? Better yet, search for "psychology at work" and you will find a plethora of books on the topic. Well, perhaps not. It depends on what you're looking for. Are you hoping to find out about psychological insights into the *general wellbeing* of employees in a modern organization, then you will indeed find plenty of food for thought. The type of psychology that deals with improving performance, motivation, job satisfaction, safety, health, and well-being, is called "Industrial (, Work) and Organizational psychology" – IO or IWO for short. That is not what this book is about, per se. Most of these topics will be touched on in relationship to various psychological aspects discussed in this work, but we will also venture beyond what is discussed in books about IO.

If you're looking for practical application of psychological insights in your *everyday interaction* with colleagues, helpful information becomes scarce. Pseudoscientific piffle at the level of astrology is plentiful, but do you really want to risk your professional career on believing rubbish? It is a much safer bet to pursue the proven psychological science.

A Psychologist

If you're coming from the psychology end of the spectrum, then you might be looking for ways to apply your knowledge in practical ways in a modern business environment. You will find plenty of hooks in this work to find out how your knowledge of the mind can be helpful and valuable for any modern organization.

Science in the Modern Workplace

What this book aims to do is to collect and present a number of core proven facts in the field of psychology which most leading scientists in the field agree upon and then outline what these findings mean in the particular environment of the modern workplace. Therein lies the difference with the topics that you will find in the average *Intro Psych* that psychology students start their careers with. The modern business angle that this work takes, illustrates the practical appliance of the psychological theories that are well known within the psychology community, but often less so outside of it.

This Book

The strength of this work lies in the linking of deep knowledge of modern-day business and organizations, based on decades of firsthand experience and study, with clear-cut scientifically backed-up widely professionally recognized psychology. As a bonus, the book mixes in succinct overviews of the recent histories of both psychology and modern-day work, which provide a helpful basis for a deeper understanding of *why* we currently do things the way we do them in our modern work environments, and why changing that is not an easy enterprise. The stories of both business and science are peppered with practical anecdotes to keep things lively and recognizable for anyone who spends time in a modern workplace anywhere on our globe.

Keep reading to find out more about the intriguing cutting-edge between the everyday workplace experience and scientifically proven psychology...

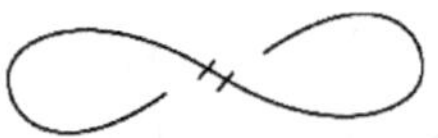

Introduction – Your Personal Use of the Book

Before you dive right in, here are some thoughts on how you could use this book to your best personal advantage.

Cover to Cover

I wrote the book to inform you, the reader, about *proven psychology* and how to make proper use of that knowledge in your *daily work environment*. I invite you to read the book cover to cover as one big story. There is a purposeful intent to the order of both the chapters and the segments within the chapters.

Short Summary

First, be gone with the falsehoods – know what nonsense is spread and what the actual facts are. Then we'll turn to the proven psychology. We start small, with the *self* – about how we function as an individual. After that, we'll dive into the interpersonal relationships – about how we interact with each other. This is the biggest chunk of the book since it relates the most to our work environments, where interaction is key. We'll also look at what we can borrow from psychological therapy to apply at work. And then we'll have a peek at things to come – how can psychology help us with future challenges in modern organizations?

Changing the Order

After almost finishing two chapters of this book, I realized that I was writing something *I* would like to start with. Given my no doubt peculiar taste in history and background, I first wrote the chapters on how psychology and work came to be what they are today. I then realized that most of you would probably like to dive into the nitty-gritty of popular psychology straight away.

I switched things around and now the book starts with popular myths, misunderstandings, and outright falsehoods. That should catch your attention right off the bat! For those of you that *are* interested in a deeper understanding of how psychology and work as we know it today took shape, don't fret, you will meet the earlier writings as chapters six and seven.

Reference Book

Even though you can easily read the book cover to cover, you can also use it as a *reference book*. Every segment within a chapter is a standalone piece of information that deals with one aspect of psychology.

That's also the reason for me to include both a straightforward and an elaborate content overview at the start of the book. In the elaborate overview, every segment about a certain psychological aspect is mentioned, so that you can easily look it up if you only want to read something about that particular topic.

Multiple Books in One

I'm very well aware that I could easily have split this book into several smaller books, but I just didn't want to do that. I could, for instance, have split the myth handling from the proven psychology, or I could have left out the history chapters altogether and created something different from that material. But, I felt all this information belonged together to give you a complete overview of what psychology entails and how it touches our work and can be of good use in our work environments.

Awareness

Speaking of being aware, if there is one thing I would like to emphasize before you flip the page, then it is the value of *awareness*. I understand the need for practical solutions. In today's ever-faster moving environments, we would like to see issues resolved as quickly as possible. And not just half resolved but fully resolved.

Believe you me, I'm just like that, with little patience and a whole-hearted belief that everything is resolvable. That's why it might be hard to swallow that sometimes, there is no quick solution available. We will see in this book that science hasn't figured out everything completely yet, or that scientists can differ in opinion.

Sometimes we understand the *issue* we face thoroughly, but we still can't find a fireproof *solution* anyway. For instance, we all suffer from *biases*, which influence our *behavior*, and sometimes negatively. I, nor anyone else, can tell you how to completely get rid of biases, but if you're *aware* of the biases and their influence, you can *actively* think about them, and steer your thoughts in other directions, and thus change your behavior accordingly. It's not a quick snappy solution and it certainly won't work for all, all of the time, but you are provided a proper direction to go on.

The mere *awareness* of the existence of psychological processes and their influences should give you the confidence to face them and perhaps even use them to your advantage.

With that, I say, off to the popular *clickbait*...

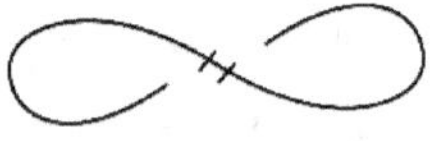

Chapter One – Beware the Nonsense

In hindsight, when I became interested in psychology through my work as a coach, I had no idea what psychology was exactly about. I supposed it had something to do with how the brain works and that if you studied the brain you could find ways to manipulate it. Now that would come in handy in my line of work!

I Coach People

As an Agile coach, I coach organizations to be able to respond to changes in the world more swiftly and to do so by inspecting and adapting iteratively, thus improving the way they operate continuously.

Even though the Agile movement originated in the software development world, the whole idea behind Agile is to make the *entire* organization nimble, not just the IT department. All too often the buck stops there however and that's what we self-proclaimed agilists call a *suboptimal* solution. This hindrance has proven to be an important catalyst in my search for more knowledge about the inner workings of the human mind.

When I say, "I coach organizations", I really mean, I coach *people* who work in organizations. Whenever you coach an organization or a team, you inevitably address the individuals within that group. Some might be willing – and able – to change and be part of the so-called *transformation* from a traditional to an Agile way of working, where others will for one reason or another work against the transformation you champion. How do you then – as an outside coach without any executive power – reach the unwilling individual and *make* them change? That eternal coaching struggle pushed me towards picking human brains and hoping to find strings in there to pull.

When my questions about the inner workings of the human brain reached a level at which I just *had* to learn more than I could figure out from online searches, I started my scholarly journey into psychology with an online course at the University of Cambridge called "Applying psychology to the workplace". I thought the title quite neatly summed up what I was looking for. Little did I know that this approach was contemplating psychology mostly from the *human resources* perspective. Not that the course wasn't useful to me, on the contrary, I learned a great deal about employee wellbeing, motivation, and satisfaction. I was also introduced to *the Hawthorne experiments* which I will discuss later on about what makes us more productive. But to be clear, this book is not in particular about *that* sort of "psychology at work".

Bluntly put, what I was looking for was a way to manipulate the people I was coaching into behaving as I saw fit from an Agile transformation perspective. And I wasn't there yet.

Sucking It All Up

After my online course at Cambridge, I enrolled in multiple online courses that talked about *the lizard brain* (fight, freeze, and flight modes), the workings of the left and right hemispheres of the brain, mirror neurons, motivational talks, "reading" people, manipulating your own and other people's thoughts, et cetera. I sucked it all up and loved it even more. Finally, I was learning things about manipulating people's minds!

After a while, however, I felt hesitations about some of the things being told. I live by the age-old adagium, if it sounds too good to be true, it probably is. So I decided to dive further into the world of psychology, this time through a more elaborate online course called *Introduction to Psychology*, delivered by Professor Paul Bloom from Yale University. Now, this turned things around! Nothing about *lizard brains*, no silliness about the creative right and analytical left hemispheres of the brain, no sinister ways of forcing my colleagues into submission, no self-help mantras, and a whole new world opening up for me.

The Dunning-Kruger Effect

In 1999, David Dunning and Justin Kruger described what has become known as the *Dunning-Kruger Effect* – the *cognitive bias* in which people highly overestimate their ability in some area of expertise. I'll come back to what a cognitive bias is in the next chapter, but here's how this particular bias works in general. You learn of a field of expertise that is relatively new to you and you dive right in because you're super interested in it. You learn the basics, but you know not enough of the topic to be able to judge that it's just the basics you've learned, and instead, you think of yourself as quite the expert in this field. It isn't until a real expert points it out to you, or when you yourself truly learn more about the topic, that you can have an honest look at your own expertise and realize that you still have so much more to learn. Your confidence in your knowledge on the topic will drop to an all-time low, to the *valley of despair*. If you persevere in the learning and allow your expertise to grow, your confidence will gradually grow with it again – you will find yourself on the *slope of enlightenment*.

Your confidence will never reach the top levels it had when you thought you knew it all, but you will eventually reach the *plateau of sustainability*. Dunning and Kruger called the top level of overconfidence in combination with utter incompetence the *Peak of Mount Stupid*. In the graph below you can see the relationship between the growing level of expertise and the evolving level of confidence that goes with it.

The Dunning-Kruger Effect

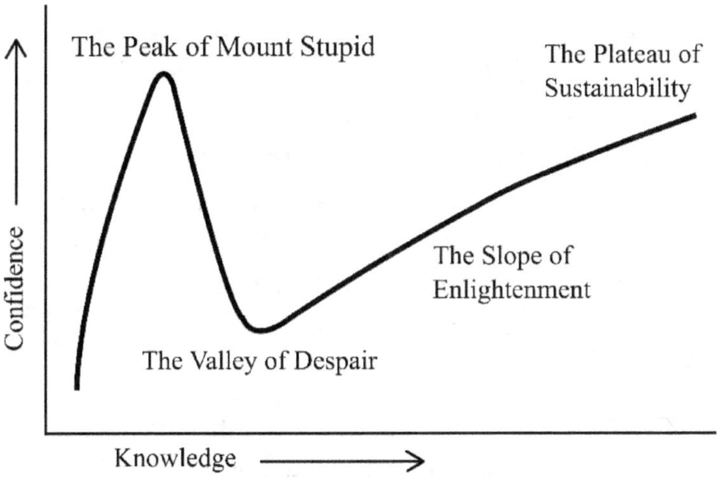

When I was following the psychology lessons of Professor Bloom, I suddenly found myself standing on the Peak of Mount Stupid. I had only learned a little bit about psychology and a lot of it false information at that. I must admit, the feeling that got hold of me was a mixture of desperate disgust and eager curiosity. I felt I had wasted too much time on pure nonsense and was angry about the garbage being so readily available without any apparent critique, and at the same time, I longed for salvation in discovering what actually *was* true and tried.

Fake News

In these days of information overload through the internet – especially through social media – it is hard to sift the good from the bad information. How can you tell the bullocks from the proven scientific facts? Especially since in recent years, politicians and their most fervent followers have pushed us into the so-called *post-truth era* in which an unsubstantiated opinion seems as important as rigorously peer-reviewed publicly published facts.

You will no doubt have (digitally) run into apparently genuine and well-versed professional sounding people – some even with degrees – telling and selling stories of scientific research that provides remedies for all kinds of problems, ranging from curing phobias to improving your chances of promotion at work or success in business. Why would you *not* believe them? For all you know, they sound pretty reasonable, *n'est-ce pas*?

Science is *Not* Just Another Opinion

When you dive into the world of science, you will find two things that might feel counterintuitive at first. One thing that struck me about Professor Bloom's lectures, is the candor with which he proclaimed to be *uncertain* about a lot of things in the field of psychology. A Yale Professor, uncertain! How about that?

It turns out that most scientists are usually pretty unsure about just about everything and they will be the first to admit that. I believe it was Albert Einstein who said, "More the knowledge, lesser the ego. Lesser the knowledge, more the ego." It will actually be hard to find a peer-reviewed publicly published article in an authoritative scientific journal which does not state that more research is needed on this or that. On the contrary, it would be rather impossible to find a paragraph in such an article that reads, "The results are in, no further research is needed in our opinion. We've got you covered, never mind any alternatives. Don't believe anything else they try to tell you, now or in the future – this is it".

Secondly, whenever a scientist has the audacity to make a new claim, their peers take a huge sledgehammer to the new theory and start slamming it with a vicious fervor until there is nothing left of it. Or, when the smoke clears, they pretty much agree that the claim might actually hold. That is until the next smart-ass comes along with a new theory that totally contradicts this one. And that new theory will then subsequently be treated in the same unforgiving manner.

The good thing about this relentless behavior is that the international scientific community has thus built a self-controlling mechanism that ensures the highest quality of proven and agreed-upon theories at any given time.

The shocking side of this way of working is not the latter sledgehammer part, but rather the former part about scientists being so unsure about most things. Being uncertain does not go over well in conversations with people who are very sure about what they have to say, even if it flies directly in the face of simple reason and logic. Needless to say, we see that on a daily basis nowadays - on the news, mostly from the world of politics, and on our social media feeds.

It becomes tragic when opinions are opposed to the facts upon which most scientists agree, like with climate change. Most scientists who have anything worthwhile to add to the conversation about it will tell you that climate change is real and that a substantial part of it is induced by human activity. You can bet your ass that if more than 97 percent of the planet's scientists agree on this, it is real. These people will have scrutinized each other's work thoroughly to find the smallest holes in it. Not because they don't believe their peers, but this is just how they work. No hard feelings, just hard work.

To see these agreed-upon facts then be cast aside by powerful politicians as "just another opinion", is not just cringeworthy, it is both heartbreaking *and* utterly dangerous.

No Harm, No Foul... Right?

Much of this work contradicts what you will find out there in the wild, in social media, in regular media, and even in very expensive business training. People seem eager to adopt good-sounding theories and remedies to sometimes serious issues without knowing an ounce about their *viability* or *reliability*. It's often hard to figure out if there truly is any scientific basis for a claim or not, but for a first hunch all it takes is a simple online search for "[theory or remedy name] + debunked" and you might find a plethora of scientific evidence against the theory or remedy.

You might wonder – well, even if a theory or remedy is not proven scientifically, does that matter? No harm, no foul, right? *Wrong*.

There are good reasons to be very skeptical about unsubstantiated claims about psychology. In the introduction of their work, *50 Great Myths of Popular Psychology*, Professors Lilienfeld, Lynn, Ruscio, and Beyerstein describe three main reasons why we should be wary of false psychology prophets.

For one, psychological myths can have *real-life* consequences. For instance in court, if a judge or jury believes that an eye-witness remembers certain events as if they're watching a video in their mind, then the verdict might be skewed in the wrong direction (memory works differently). Or if your employer (falsely) believes *punishment* will help change long-term behavior, you're in for a ride!

Secondly, fake psychological news can have adverse *indirect* consequences. If you believe the unfounded nonsense of a motivational coach and spend thousands on courses and sessions, you won't be able to spend that hard-earned money elsewhere. (On top of that, neither will you get the fantastic results you were promised, which has its own adverse consequences.)

And thirdly, the acceptance of psychological baloney can reduce your *critical thinking* in other fields. If you wholeheartedly believe the wonder therapist that claims you can *think* yourself out of a serious mental illness with *positive thoughts*, what's to stop you from casting aside expert advice on, for instance, global warming or a worldwide pandemic?

Popular Myths

Before we dive into the scientifically proven psychology next chapter, let's become aware of the BS that is being upheld – knowingly and unknowingly – and examine some of the more popular psychological myths, ranging from long-held misunderstandings to more recent baseless claims.

We only use 10% of our brainpower

You still hear people make the claim every now and then that we leave a lot of our brainpower unused and only use 10% of what we actually could be using. Its origins go back almost a century. In 1936, journalist Lowell Thomas wrote the preface to a best-selling self-help book, Dale Carnegie's *How to Win Friends and Influence People*, in which he attributed the 10% claim to one of the most revered psychologists of all time, American William James (1842-1910). James, however, only once said that he doubted that average persons achieve more than about 10% of their *intellectual potential*, which was a wild claim on James' part about an undefined term.

The unfortunate popularity of the claim that we only use 10% of our brainpower received boosts from the ever uncertain scientists who claimed – especially in the early days of psychology – that they didn't know what 90% of the brain actually did.

In more recent years, neuroscience has shown that *neurons* are the cells that seem to do most of the hard work of our brains and that they only make up about 10% of our brains. Not that the other cells – like the supporting *glial* cells – are sitting idly by, but the 10% is – again – a very unfortunate coincidence.

On top of it all, some people contribute the *10% of our brainpower* idea to none other than Albert Einstein – but this contribution looks to be totally baseless.

From an evolutionary perspective, the 10% idea makes no sense. Even though our brain makes up only about 2 to 3% of our body weight, it does consume over 20% of the oxygen we breathe. It doesn't make much practical sense for mother nature to evolve such an energy squandering organ and not use more than 10% of it. The reality behind the myth is that we use many different areas of our brain to perform even the simplest of tasks and no part of our brains goes unused. Modern brain scans, like fMRIs, have shown this conclusively.

There are left-brain and right-brain people

A popular theory is that people are either left-brained or right-brained, meaning that one side of their brain is dominant. According to this theory, if your *left* side is dominant, you're mostly *analytical* and *methodical* in your thinking. On the other hand, if your *right* side is dominant, you tend to be more *creative* or *artistic*. Unfortunately, this false idea has taken root in many organizations. It is often brought up in conversations about a *left-brained management team* versus a *right-brained marketing team*, or a *left-brained project manager* versus a *right-brained software development team*. The problem with this and many other myths is that there is a very small grain of truth to it, but certainly not as huge and as precise as many take it to be.

The small grain of truth stems from research that was done from the 1960s onwards by 1981 Nobel Prize-winning neuropsychologist Roger Sperry and one of his students, Michael Gazzaniga. They studied patients whose brain was quite literally split in half. As scientists figured out in the 1960s, patients who suffered from severe epilepsy could – as a last resort – have the bridge between the two halves of their brain, the *corpus callosum*, physically cut to ease their suffering. At first, the patients seemed to be functioning quite normally after the procedure, but soon the neuroscientists figured out that the two halves of their brains worked separately side by side without knowing anything about what the other half knew or did. Earlier psychologists already figured – by observing patients with specific brain damage – that our brains prefer to do certain tasks in the left hemisphere of the brain and others on the right side. Now, Sperry and later Gazzaniga had real evidence.

For instance, they'd have a patient stare straight ahead while showing them a picture of an apple to their left eye only. You need to know that the optic nerve leading from your *left* eyeball to your brain goes across to the *right* hemisphere. They found that these patients weren't able to tell what they were seeing. This coincided with the assumption that language is processed in the left hemisphere. Even if the patient was subsequently given an apple in their left hand – still without the right eye seeing it – they would know they had just seen the same thing in the picture, but they still weren't able to *say* it was an apple.

Even more interesting were experiments where the two hemispheres were shown two different pictures, for instance, a chicken to the left eye and a car to the right. Then the patient's left hand had to pick a card that had to be associated with the first picture. Let's say they picked a card with the picture of an egg (because of the chicken that was seen by the right hemisphere). Now the patient was asked to explain the choice of the card with the picture of an egg. The left hemisphere – better at language – answered. Remember, the left hemisphere had no clue as to why the right hemisphere picked the picture of an egg since the left hemisphere had only seen the picture of a car. The interesting thing is that the patients invariably *made up* stories about the choice that was made! In this case, the patient might have concocted a story – with the *left* hemisphere mind you – about needing the car to get some eggs from the grocery store. So far for the *analytical left* versus the *creative right* that is so often propelled in organizations still!

Most of us do not have our *corpus callosum* cut, so our brain halves cooperate just fine. When it comes to language processing, the left hemisphere is usually best at processing the *grammar*, but the right is usually best at *intonation* and *emphasis*. To understand language, both hemispheres work closely together. If you hear someone say something to you, one part of the brain analyses what is being said and what that literally means, while another part extracts the emotions of the speaker from the tone of voice, the posture, et cetera. All this information combined gives the listener a true sense of what the speaker actually meant to say. What neuroscientists have found – for instance through making fMRIs (brain scans) – is that in normal brains, the two halves *always* work together in harmony and one side is *not* dominant over the other.

While our brain seems to have a slight preference for certain physical areas to do certain work, that does not appear to come from a point of necessity. Different parts of the brain work closely together to the point of inseparability. When a certain part of the brain is damaged, other parts of the brain are often able to take over whatever that part seems to be specialized in, also crossing the border between the left and right hemispheres. Also keep in mind that for a lot of people, what we consider to be left-brain preferences, actually take place in their right hemisphere and vice versa. For instance, 95% of right-handed people have a preference to process language with their left hemisphere, while only 70% of left-handed people have a preference to process language with the same hemisphere. The others either prefer the right hemisphere or divide the process over both hemispheres.

This all goes to show that sometimes a small piece of truth can lead to a big unfounded claim.

The female brain differs significantly from the male brain

A popular myth that indulges the sexists amongst us, is that men and women have very different kinds of brains – or at least that their brains are used very differently. In 1992, American pop psychologist John Gray (not to be confused with British philosopher John Gray) wrote the famous book, *Men are from Mars, Women are from Venus*, with which he meant to say that men and women think and communicate quite differently, which in turn supposedly causes a lot of friction in households, at work, and in society at large. Gray hit a nerve apparently since his book sales in the US in the nineties were second only to the Bible!

The strange thing is that neither Gray nor other pop psychologists who took his claims and ran with them have conducted any research to back these claims up. Numerous scientists on the other hand *have* done the homework and sought to find if there was any truth to the ideas about male and female brain differences.

Again there is a grain of truth to be found on the basis of it all. The fact is that men's brains are *on average* slightly larger than women's brains – with the stress on *"on average"*. There are still plenty of women who have bigger brains than most men. There are even brain parts that differ significantly in size. The *hippocampus*, which is heavily involved in our (spatial) memory, is usually larger in women, but the *amygdala*, dealing with memory, decision making, and emotional responses, is typically larger in men. (Yes, you read that right, the part that deals with *emotional responses* is typically larger in men!) Sometimes even specific sub-parts of brain parts work differently. Emotional memories seem to trigger the left part of the amygdala more in women, but the right part more in men.

In spite of all these – and more – physical differences, there's one conclusion that can't be simply drawn, and that is that *physical* differences imply *behavioral* differences. Gray takes his reasoning even further from the true physical differences by alluding to differences that don't even exist. He claims, for instance, that men use a particular part of one hemisphere to accomplish a certain task, while women utilize both hemispheres to accomplish the same. This would explain the idea that men are more focused and single-minded, while women are better at multitasking. As we've seen in previous paragraphs, modern brain scans (fMRIs) show that even the simplest of tasks light up our entire brain and that both hemispheres always work together quite closely. And this is no different for men than it is for women.

The scientists that *did* do their homework, researched some tenacious sexist prejudices, for instance, whether women talk more than men, whether men interrupt others more often, and if women are more perceptive of nonverbal cues than men. They used a metric called Cohen's *d*, after statistician and psychologist Jacob Cohen (1923-1998) who made it popular. Basically, the lower the *d*, the lesser the difference. For instance, looking at physical aggression, the *d* is about 0.60, with men being more aggressive than women. For height, the *d* is about 1.70, with men being a lot taller than women. So, what about the homework? The combined results of 73 studies into how much people talk, found a *d* of 0.11, with women being slightly more talkative than men. The difference is however so slightly that it's barely noticeable in real life. Psychologist Matthias Mehl and his colleagues even found through research that both men and women utter about 16,000 words a day. Do men interrupt more often than women? 53 studies say the *d* is about 0.15, and again the difference would be hardly noticeable. Also, when women are in charge, *they* interrupt more and talk a lot more. How about the perception of nonverbal cues? My wife certainly lets me know – after parties or family gatherings – that I didn't pick up on any of her nonverbal cues, and indeed, Cohen's *d* goes up to 0.40, meaning there *is* a significant difference noticeable. A small grain is found.

Neuroscientist Larry Cahill explains in his 2006 paper *Why sex matters for neuroscience* why we shouldn't be *too* politically correct about differences between sexes. Some psychological conditions are heavily skewed towards either males or females. Autism, for instance, is a lot more prevalent in men, while depression is more common for women. Also, Alzheimer's disease seems to impact women heavier than it does men. To ignore or evade sex differences could have disastrous effects on healthcare.

Even though there are real differences between both physical appearances and behavior of men's and women's brains, the fact remains that the similarities outweigh the differences by a landslide. Some scientists have even suggested that the differences are only there to create more similar *outcomes*. This is called the *compensation theory* and could explain why men and women can accomplish the same tasks while showing different brain activity patterns.

The idea that men have different brains from women stems mostly from sexist cultural indoctrination than reality. Studies have shown that if you tell women they are worse at math than men before they take a test, they actually do worse, whereas, if you tell them there is no real difference in being good at math between men and women, they perform equally well.

In short, in a work situation, we'd all be wise to assume and radiate that men and women are equal to any task. Individual differences are more likely to be just that – *individual* – rather than gender-related.

We have a lizard brain inside our modern brain

In the 1960s, American physician and neuroscientist Paul D. MacLean (1913-2007) formulated a model about the evolution of the brain which he explained in detail in his 1990 book *The Triune Brain in Evolution*. MacLean propounds that the *triune brain* consists of the *reptilian complex*, the *limbic system*, and the *neocortex*, each independently conscious parts of the brain that were sequentially added to the brain over the course of evolution. In the early days of neuroanatomy, scientists like MacLean believed that the forebrains of birds and reptiles were dominated by the part of the brain that is physically located near the bottom of the brain, the *basal ganglia.* This *reptilian complex* – or *lizard brain* – is responsible for instinctual behaviors like those involved with aggression, self-preservation, and fear of the unknown. The most famous example coming out of this idea is the *fight, flight,* or *freeze* model that says people have one of these basic responses to impetuous events – physically and/or verbally. Think of a robbery and what someone might do as a response. One person would fight off the robber, while another would be quick on their feet and get away, while a third person might just stand there and do nothing at all. In a work environment, someone might be confronted by an aggressive boss and have an instinctual response to this verbal attack. One might rebut the boss in an equally aggressive manner, where someone else might evade the boss for the coming days by slipping into another office room or even the toilet, while another might fall totally silent – not able to move and say anything.

The *limbic system* – a term that MacLean introduced in 1952 – consists of several parts of the brain that are interconnected and responsible for the motivation and feelings around *social* and *nurturing* behavior. MacLean proposed the limbic system arose during the early days of the first mammals. Amongst the brain parts that are part of the limbic system are the *amygdalae* – heavily involved in decision making and memory – and the *hippocampus* – heavily involved in (spatial) memory.

MacLean insisted the *neocortex* is found only in highly evolved mammals – especially humans – and he considered this the latest addition to the brain in evolution, responsible for language, abstraction, planning, and perception.

Since MacLean proposed his lizard brain ideas, neuroscience has brought a lot more details to light about the physical parts of the brain. It turns out that the *basal ganglia* – the *reptilian complex* – are found in *all* modern vertebrates, including fish, amphibians, birds, reptiles, and mammals. Also, research into animal behavior has shown that the behavior of neither birds nor reptiles is as basic and simple as MacLean's theory suggests. Crows and parrots, for instance, possess highly sophisticated cognitive abilities that contradict MacLean's ideas of the *lizard brain*. The idea that the *neocortex* was the most recent addition to the brain and most prevalent in humans has taken a blow since the neocortex was found to be already present in the most primitive of mammals. Even though non-mammals do not have a neocortex, they do possess so-called *pallial* regions that function in a similar manner. Moreover, mammals and non-mammals alike have a *telencephalon* or *cerebrum* – the biggest part of the brain – that makes neuroanatomical connections just like the *neocortex* does, thus mediating in functions like perception, learning and memory, decision making, and conceptual thinking. The *compensation theory*, as mentioned when discussing the differences between male and female brains, could very well be applied to differences in brain structure between species – different physical features could result in the same accomplishments.

Coming back to the *fight*, *flight*, or *freeze* responses, modern brain scans show us that much of the brain lights up when *any* thinking, analysis, or decision making is happening, thus eradicating the idea that only a small part of the brain – the *lizard brain* – would be responsible for such a basic response.

The popular *lizard brain* idea is a decades-old concept that oversimplifies and at least partially inaccurately explains the working and evolution of the brain.

The exciting field of neuroscience is the key to all psychological answers

You wouldn't know it from reading the many articles related to neuroscience in the last few decades, but neuroscience itself dates back thousands of years. The ancient Egyptians already had some notion of the physical anatomy of the nervous system. To be precise about it, the nervous system consists of more than just the brain. The *central nervous system* is defined as the brain together with the spinal cord, while the rest of the network of neurons throughout the body is called the *peripheral nervous system.*

Neuron

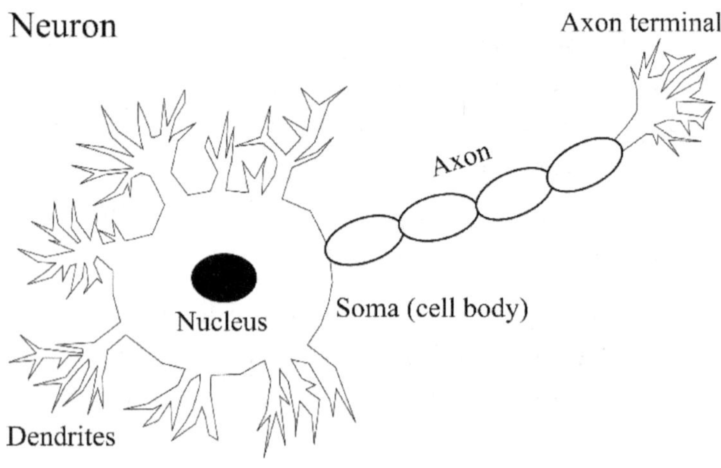

      Typical neurons consist of a cell body (called *soma*), with a nucleus, dendrites, and a single axon with axon terminals. A soma uses its dendrites to receive signals. The signals are sent through the axon – which can be as long as one meter or more in a human body – to the axon terminals. There the signals go through a synapse to another cell, which could be another neuron, a muscle cell, a gland cell, et cetera. Thus, a signal can start in your brain, go through several different neurons, and end up in your toes. Neurons can also be bi-directional or even multi-directional, sending signals from the brain, to the brain, and towards other neurons. To give you an idea of the vastness of the nervous system, the human brain contains around one hundred billion neurons and one hundred trillion synapses.

The work of Luigi Galvani (1737-1798) ushered in the pre-modern era of neuroscience in which it became clear that the system of neurons and muscles work through the use of *electricity*. Later it was determined the signal processing is partly *electrical*, partly *chemical*. During the second half of the twentieth century neuroscience really took flight due to advances in molecular biology and computer techniques. Since the 1990s, the use of fMRI scans (*functional Magnetic Resonance Imaging* scans) has allowed scientists to monitor which areas of the nervous system are activated. Basically it works through the scan of blood flow. Luckily enough, the activation of neurons coincides with blood flow towards those neurons. The fMRI scan sees where the blood flows, and thus, where the action takes place. One surprising fact the neuroscientists found is that much of the brain lights up on scans, whatever we're doing or thinking, indicating that much of our brain is at work most of the time.

Before fMRI scans showed the overall busyness of the brain, many believed that certain parts of the brain were very specialized in certain processing and acted in solitude. French scientist Paul Broca (1824-1880) was one of the first to notice a specialization of a small area of the frontal lobe in language. He even got that part named after him, it is known as *Broca's area.* We know now that even though at least some specialization takes place, it is not absolute. Language, for instance, is processed throughout the brain, with different areas having different focuses – like *meaning* or *intonation.*

What can be seen as a successful exploration of the physical brain does not translate one on one to an equally successful exploration of the relationship between what is observed physically in the brain and on the outside in behavior. Despite the revealing findings, neuroscience is not mind-reading. What we see on fMRI scans is clear but confusing. Our brains differ in how they work from day to day, or even from minute to minute. Just when you think you've found a relation between observed behavior and a certain part of the brain, the relationship disappears and reappears somewhere else in another brain part the next second. Moreover, my brain does not function the same as your brain – where you might observe a relation between activity and behavior in my brain, you're likely to *not* find the same relation in your brain.

Sometimes the wish is father to the thought. Despite all of the insights into our physical brain that neuroscience has given us, not every aspect of the working of our mind has been explained by it – many questions still remain unanswered, and many more have arisen exactly because of these new insights.

Mirror neurons give us empathy and humanity

In the 1990s, Italian neurophysiologist Giacomo Rizzolatti and his colleagues were researching brain activity in Macaque monkeys. What they found – by accident – is that certain neurons were activated when Rizzolatti's colleague Leonardo Fogassi reached out to get some raisins for the monkeys. The same neurons were activated when the monkeys themselves reached out for raisins. Hence the name that was given to these types of neurons – *mirror neurons*.

There has been much controversy surrounding these mirror neurons from the beginning. In 2000, San Diego neuroscientist Vilayanur Ramachandran took the discussion to a whole new level when he predicted that mirror neurons would do for psychology what DNA did for biology – namely provide numerous explanations for previously totally mysterious behavior. Ramachandran carried things even further when he claimed in 2011 that mirror neurons underlie *empathy*, accelerated the evolution of the brain, and even prompted the great leap forward in human culture that happened around 60,000 years ago, when we started to use more tools and create more sophisticated art. Others, like neuroscience author Rita Carter, have introduced the idea that some people have "broken mirror neurons", like autistic people, who often lack empathy.

In reality, while all these hypotheses sound pretty awesome, not much of their working is backed up by research or research outcomes. Much of the research has been done with monkeys, which makes the idea that mirror neurons make us "more human" a bit ridiculous in itself. On top of that, the research shows that there are apparently many different types of mirror neurons. Some respond to seeing live movement, others also to movement on video, yet others to sound, or touch. Also, sometimes it seems not to be individual neurons at work, but rather a whole system that mirrors what is observed – for instance when you see someone in pain, then you (probably) feel the pain too, and not just with a few mirror neurons.

The idea that autistic people have a *broken mirror system* was itself broken down in 2011 when Morton Ann Gernsbacher concluded from numerous studies that autistic people have no problem understanding other people's actions and that they show normal imitation abilities and reflexes.

The notion of mirror neurons has a popular following, even amongst some scholars. The mirror neurons seem to play a role in our social behavior, like empathy and understanding someone else's intentions, but to which degree is still up for debate. Some scientists, like Alfonse Caramazza from Harvard University, openly doubt if we have *any* mirror neurons at all – if they even exist (in humans). In short, don't put all your money on mirror neurons just yet, the evidence is scant.

Brain-training will make you smart

During the 2000s, several computer game makers claimed to make you smarter if you trained your brain with their games. By exercising with the games on a regular basis, you would be able to improve a wide range of cognitive abilities in real life. The training would benefit your memory, your speed of thinking, your scholastic results, and it would even benefit children with developmental cognitive disorders and help prevent or at least delay dementia and general mental decline in the elderly.

First a short sidestep about intelligence, which we'll explore more in-depth in the next chapter. Generally speaking, intelligence is divided into *fluid* intelligence and *crystallized* intelligence. Crystallized intelligence refers to your knowledge of facts, which grows over your lifetime. Fluid intelligence alludes to your ability to solve *new* problems, unrelated to your accumulated knowledge. What these brain-training games mostly aim for, is to grow your fluid intelligence. They do this with exercises created to target your so-called *working memory*. More about the different types of memory in the next chapter, but basically your working memory is what holds your current thoughts. It typically holds only about seven chunks of information and lasts only a few seconds. If you don't repeat the chunks in your working memory, they quickly fade away. (If you repeat them long enough, they become encoded in your more permanent long-term memory.) The short-term or working memory has been shown to have a close relationship with fluid intelligence, hence the idea that if you improve your working memory, you increase your intelligence.

The modicum of truth can be found in research by Swedish scientist Torkel Klingsberg in 2002, who found improvements in working memory in children with ADHD after only four weeks of working memory exercises. Not only that, but the children also improved their abstract thinking abilities as well as their fluid intelligence. Another well-known 2008 study by Swiss researcher Susanne Jaeggi showed that indeed, working memory training increased fluid intelligence in young healthy adults.

In 2010, British researcher Adrian Owen and his colleagues conducted an extensive six-week study with more than 11,000 participants on the effects of brain-training. They divided the participants in three groups – one that engaged in general cognitive training and practised tests of memory, attention, visuospatial processing and mathematics, another group that received more focused training with tests of reasoning, planning and problem solving, and one control group that received no brain-training. The results showed no evidence for any generalized improvements in cognitive abilities, for any of the groups. They also looked at gender and age, but no matter what, all changes in performance were negligible.

In 2013, Norwegian scientist Monica Melby-Lervåg and British researcher Charles Hume concluded – after a meta-analysis of 23 studies into working memory training – that the only achievement noticeable is a short-term gain on working memory performance on tests that are the same or very similar to the ones used in the training exercises. Psychologists call this *near transfer*, as opposed to *far transfer*, which would be the case if any positive cognitive effects would have been seen in real-life situations – as in, different from the tests that were used. But they found no evidence that working memory training produces generalizable gains to any other skills that they also tested.

Numerous studies since have indeed shown that any training-related improvements may not even generalize to other tasks that relate to similar cognitive functions.

Although brain-training never seems to hurt and might even be considered a fun form of entertainment, psychologists point out that the best way to exercise your brain is a healthy combination of physical exercise, learning new skills, and socializing.

Despite the alluring idea of becoming smarter by playing games, you only become slightly better for a short period at exactly what you train. Doing brain-training computer games makes you better at doing brain-training computer games, but it will not increase your intelligence in general.

10,000 hours of training will make you an expert in any field

In 1993, Swedish psychologist Karl Anders Ericsson (1947-2020) researched how many hours violinists had practiced to reach their level of expertise. It turned out that the highest tier of violinists had practiced about 10,000 hours, which was more than the number of hours practiced by the lower tiers. Ericsson and his colleagues concluded that characteristics once believed to reflect innate talent are actually the result of intense practice for at least ten years.

Journalist Malcolm Gladwell (1963) described the *10,000 hours of practice rule* in his bestselling book

Outliers, declaring the 10,000 hours "the magic number of greatness". Even though Ericsson distanced himself from this "popularized and simplistic view" of his work, the idea was picked up by people in sports and business alike and projected onto their world and has thus – unfortunately – taken root.

Numerous studies since have shown that in fact, practice is very much overrated. American assistant professor of psychology Brooke Macnamara and colleagues have done extensive meta-analysis to find what studies have said about the amount of practice and its influence on performance. In 2014, they examined 88 papers that looked at practice times and found that deliberate practice attributes for only 26% to better performance in games, 21% in music, 18% in sports, 4% in education, and around 1% in professions and elite athletes. Macnamara specifically points to a study of chess players which showed that some were able to qualify for the World Chess Federation title after only 3,000 hours of practice, while others needed more than 20,000 hours. Besides the training, big indicators of successful performance are intelligence, the age at which you start training, the type of training, whether you have a coach or not, and your working memory capacity.

The *10,000 hours of training to become an expert* idea was never intended to be taken as far as it is being applied today in business and sports. Research has shown that it actually isn't true and that there are many variables at work to create an expert. The amount of practice plays a role that is sometimes relatively large, but often only marginal.

People learn better through their preferred learning style

This is a tricky one, I must admit. We all probably have the *feeling* we are better at learning new skills through a certain way – for instance, by seeing, hearing, or feeling (physically enacting) how to perform them. There are literally thousands of books, articles, websites, conference presentations, theses, et cetera, that allude to the benefits of aligning a teacher's *teaching style* to a student's *learning style*. The idea that students learn new information *better* by learning it through their preferred learning style is also very popular amongst teachers. They will certainly – and correctly – notice that different students experience enlightenment from different approaches. One student might respond to an image much better than to spoken words, which the teacher might take into account the next time when trying to explain something new to the same student.

There are several issues with the supposed benefits of matching *teaching style* to *learning style*. For one, different theories apply different learning and teaching styles. I already mentioned the popular *visual, auditory*, and *kinesthetic* categories, but others use a classification into *activists*, *reflectors*, *theorists*, and *pragmatists* (Honey & Mumford's model), and yet others use different classifications altogether. So, depending on the model you adopt, your teaching style would be different for the same student – which doesn't make sense at all.

Secondly, there is no reliable and viable way to figure out a student's learning style. The biggest problem here is context. Would you prefer learning how to drive a car just by watching images? Probably not. Most people would want to actually hop in a car and get to feel what it's like to drive around. On the other hand, would you like to learn about concentration camps by experiencing one? I think for most, reading or hearing about them would suffice, perhaps along with seeing images or video. So, there you go, different context, different preferred learning style.

Then there is the question, does it actually work? Do students perform better when the teacher adjusts their style to the student's preferred learning style? Since the 1970s, at least as many studies have failed to show the relation as have supported it. The mixed results make sense if you take into account that certain teaching styles offer better results regardless of the student's preferred learning style – so good performance is the result of a *better* teaching style, not a *matching* teaching style.

And last but not least, is it even possible to train teachers to adjust to the preferred learning styles of their students? The evidence for this is weak at best, and inconsistent mostly. So, even if you wanted to, it would be hard to match the teacher's style to the student's style anyway.

What does seem to work best, is to create a teaching style that benefits *all* students, no matter their preferred learning style. The use of a combination of different styles, like images with spoken words, seems to work well. Also, there's solid evidence that taking quizzes in between receiving information helps you remember the information better – which would again benefit all types of students.

Researchers caution that the myth of matching *learning* and *teaching* styles might do a lot of harm. Students – anybody who studies – might think they are limited in the way they learn things and they might even avoid learning certain skills because they assume up-front that it wouldn't match the way their brains work. Also, outside the classroom – in real life – you don't always have the choice of picking your preferred style, you'll simply have to deal with whatever is presented to you. If you then think that you won't be able to learn because of the teaching style that is being applied, you'll sell yourself short. For optimal results, students and teachers alike should realize they have a full repertoire of styles to choose from, depending on the context.

With a growth mindset, we are able to reach unknown heights

In 2006, Carol Dweck (1946) published her now famous book, "Mindset: The New Psychology of Success". Her work on the attitude or belief of people towards the innateness or malleability of intelligence and other traits has caused quite a stir in the business world. Dweck maintains that people can roughly be divided into two groups, one with what she calls a *fixed mindset*, and one with a *growth mindset*. People with a *fixed mindset* mostly believe that we are born with certain abilities and that these stay basically the same throughout our lives. People with a *growth mindset* mostly believe that we can grow our intelligence and other traits by working hard, learning, and training. She makes a point of *fixed mindset* people having a strong dislike of *failure* and *growth mindset* people enjoying failure as a chance to learn and grow. In the eyes of Dweck, a *growth mindset* is highly favorable over a *fixed mindset*.

You might recognize this idea from the *lean* and *Agile* world, where the positive approach towards *failure* is advocated strongly, even encouraged. "Fail fast," is the motto that espouses the idea that if you put your product out in the market very quickly – perhaps even before you consider it to be ready enough to become a great success – you will receive valuable feedback from real end-users. In other words, you will hear very quickly what they don't like about your product, which could be considered a failure by some, but on the other hand grants you the opportunity to act upon that feedback quickly and adjust accordingly.

Throughout her book, Dweck makes comparisons between what a *growth mindset* person thinks about a certain situation, as opposed to the – in her eyes – very limiting ways a *fixed mindset* person thinks about the same situation. For instance, when she discusses business and mindset, the example of Enron keeps popping up. Energy company Enron supposedly had a very *fixed mindset*, with a very large focus on hiring *talent*. Management consultants of the time (we're talking the nineties here), like those of McKinsey, put it bluntly as "corporate success requires the *talent mindset*". The downside of hiring only the supposedly most talented people, according to Dweck, is that they then act accordingly, and talented people don't make mistakes, now do they? Failure is not an option. The employees of Enron were basically forced into a *fixed mindset*. With nobody admitting or correcting their deficiencies, Enron's success turned sour very rapidly in 2001 and led to the largest corporate bankruptcy in U.S. history up until then. If only the higher management of Enron would have possessed a *growth mindset*, then all of this misery could have been prevented.

Or so Dweck would have us believe. In reality, it was not the covering up of mistakes that was the problem at Enron, it was *willful malice* at the hands of the executives, all the way to the top. And we have the trial results to prove that point. CEOs Kenneth Lay and Jeffrey Skilling were convicted to years in prison, together with CFO Andrew Fastow, and many other top executives at Enron, for *fraud*, *money laundering*, *insider trading*, and *conspiracy*, amongst other crimes.

This is where we start to see the cracks in the seemingly wonderful model of the *fixed* and *growth mindset*. In the meantime, numerous psychologists around the world have tried to replicate the findings of Dweck, and none have succeeded so far. Our previously introduced *scientific sledgehammer* has quite smashed the mindset theory, but again – as with personality testing – popular business interests keep it very much alive today. Once again, one could ask, what's the trouble? If businesses are willing to flush money down the drain for unchecked baloney, who cares? I wish it were that simple.

Where Dweck emphasizes that praising intelligence has the negative consequence that people start to act in accordance with the image of an intelligent person – for instance, implying not to make mistakes and not asking questions because they know everything already – critics of Dweck counter that constant praising of the supposed *ideal of a growth mindset* results in people being addressed as negative or limited when they raise the realistic boundaries of what can be achieved.

Anyone visiting larger organizations will at times have heard the terms *fixed* and *growth mindset* in meeting rooms and hallways alike. People are judged by their peers – or worse, their managers – and labeled as having a *fixed* or a *growth mindset*. Once you carry the negative label of having a *fixed mindset*, it's pretty hard to get rid of, which could have negative consequences for your career. Also, important business decisions could very well be based on all too hopeful *growth mindset* assumptions, dismissing the more cautious – but perhaps more realistic – *fixed mindset* arguments.

I agree one can achieve just as much or even more in life by working hard, learning, and training than on pure talent alone. A clear-cut example is a comparison between soccer stars Cristiano Ronaldo and Lionel Messi. Experts agree Messi is the most talented of the two, born with a silken touch and superb control of the ball, hardly matched in the sport's history. But Ronaldo works his butt off, every... single... day. He works, learns, trains, fails, and gets up again, only to come out stronger than everyone else, except for maybe that other guy, but I'll leave *that* final verdict up to you.

What is clear though, is that neither Ronaldo is without talent, nor can Messi do without training. This is key to counter the ideas of a *fixed* and a *growth mindset* since it addresses the limited reach and effects of any mindset. As Dweck admits, not everyone is the same and not everyone has it in them to become the next Einstein. In practice, however, this is *exactly* the takeaway for most people who learn about the two mindsets – what people seem to remember is that if you just put your mind to it, and work hard, you can achieve *any goal* you choose. Not only are people *labeled* where they should not be, but I've also seen people being *scrutinized* in meetings for not having the right mindset – literally for not having a *growth mindset*.

Adding to this, Ronaldo and Messi are *very close* in talent. Where Messi might have a little more, Ronaldo makes up for with hard work. But, in most larger organizations, you will find people working together who are not close in talent at all. This means situations can get very frustrating for everyone involved. I concur that no matter your mindset, you will never be able to bump up your IQ with ten points by working hard, learning, and training. You can try all you might, but you will never be able to explain Einstein's *Theory of Relativity* to a person with an IQ of

60. Trying this will very rapidly reach high levels of frustration for both the trainer and the trainee.

Moreover, I believe that an organization shouldn't even *want* to have *growth mindset* people *only* within their ranks. It's very valuable for any organization to have people present who object to wild ideas of colleagues and management alike. A little realism never hurt anybody.

The wildly popular idea of *fixed* and *growth mindsets* was proposed by Carol Dweck in 2006 but was never substantiated by other research. Besides the lack of evidence for the theory, both the labeling of people as having a *fixed* or a *growth mindset*, as well as the propagated preference for a *growth mindset* is potentially harmful for both people and business.

Personality tests are a reliable tool for hiring, firing, and setting up teams

In many business environments, personality tests considering 16 or more traits, or 16 or more personality profiles, prevail. There is an entire *personality assessment industry* worth billions of dollars and no doubt you've come across at least some of them. Two of the most famous tests are the *Myers-Briggs Type Indicator,* or *MBTI*, based on the personality types as proposed by Swiss psychiatrist Carl Jung (1875-1961), and the *DISC assessment*, based on the work of American psychologist William Moulton Marston (1893-1947), who also invented – with his wife Elizabeth – the *polygraph*, and who gave us the comic book character *Wonder Woman*. The latter test is most famous for the colors that are used to indicate a certain personality type. These colors have even become part of the lingo in many organizations. Who hasn't heard colleagues utter words along the lines of, "Peter is really blue and just can't get along with John, because he's really green." And therein lies one of the many dangers of these tests. People are stigmatized because of what comes out of such a test, taken at a particular time under particular circumstances.

Moreover, the science behind tests like these is feeble, to say the least. As we will see in the later chapter about the history of psychology, the theories of Freud and his pupil Jung have all but been debunked in later decades already. So, guess what you get with a test based on personality types, based on debunked theories? *Pseudoscience* is what you get, especially when it concerns its supposed *predictive* abilities. *Myer-Briggs* exhibits significant scientific psychometric *deficiencies*, including poor *validity*, poor *reliability*, measuring categories that are not independent, and not comprehensive. In other words, the test doesn't measure what it purports to measure, it doesn't have predictive power, it gives different results for the same person on different occasions, and it's missing key elements, like measuring *neuroticism*.

DISC

If you look into the *DISC assessment*, things get even hairier. Psychologist Marston propounded his *DISC Theory* in his book "Emotions of Normal People", in 1928. He described four quadrants along two axes, with *activity* versus *passivity* on the vertical axis, and a *favorable* versus an *antagonistic* environment on the horizontal axis. According to Marston, you then get the following options:

- *D*ominance produces activity in an antagonistic environment
- *I*nducement produces activity in a favorable environment
- *S*ubmission produces passivity in a favorable environment
- *C*ompliance produces passivity in an antagonistic environment

Marston associated colors with the four terms. He linked the color blue to Dominance, red to Inducement, yellow to Submission, and green to Compliance.

In 1956, industrial psychologist Walter Clarke (1905-1978) constructed an assessment based on Marston's *DISC Theory*. He created a *checklist* of adjectives on which he asked people to indicate descriptions that were accurate about themselves. In 1965, Clarke and others changed the test, so that instead of using a checklist, the test forced respondents to choose between two or more terms.

Meanwhile, Clarke also changed some more. He changed the I in DISC from Inducement to *Influence*, the S from Submission to *Steadiness*, and the C from Compliance to *Conscientiousness*. He also changed the colors. Dominance became red and Conscientiousness became blue, while Influence became yellow and Steadiness green.

In subsequent decades, several different companies have adopted the model and have adjusted it to suit their own interests – mostly financial – even though all of them still love to namedrop *psychologist* Marston as the source of their test. Some have adjusted the C to mean Compliant, and have kept it blue, while again others have switched things around completely, with a green D for Dominant, a red I for Inspiring, a blue S for Supportive, a yellow C for Cautious, a horizontal axis going from left to right from *task* to *people*, and a vertical axis going from bottom to top from *reserved* to *outgoing*.

Needless to say, the described chaos of meanings of letters, terms, and colors, combined with the poor validity, the poor viability, interdependence, and lack of comprehension also force the *DISC assessments* into the realm of *pseudoscience*.

Yet, personality tests like *Myer-Briggs*, *DISC*, *PAPI*, and others, are still very much in use in organizations today. HR departments depend on tests like these to hire new personnel. The question is, why would a twenty-first-century organization be spending their scarce time and money, even basing the hiring of new employees, in other words, basing their future, on *pseudoscientific claptrap*? The bittersweet and short of it is *ignorance*. Most HR departments don't have well-trained, critical psychologists in their ranks who oppose this nonsense. As a consequence, people who see other organizations use these tests, tend to submit to the idea that if a multitude of organizations worldwide uses them, well, then they must be okay (we'll talk about this psychological phenomenon called *conformity* in a later chapter). On top of that, if they read that it's all based on the work of a well-known psychologist, then the *authority bias* kicks in, and there we go. Again, more on biases in later chapters.

Moreover, some qualified psychologists do not oppose these sorts of tests and use them as a starting point for further conversation. Of course, something like the DISC assessment is so easy to apply and so easy to use in daily parlance that it's hard to weed out. You can do an online *DISC assessment* in minutes and receive your *true* color description immediately. How rich is it to know your color and politically make use of that whenever it suits you. Why would you relinquish control if you're as red as a Ferrari? It's in your personality!

I once heard a comedian say it best when he said the world is full of dumb people, together with a small number of people who are just smart enough to make good use of that.

NLP is super powerful stuff

The wildly popular *Neuro-Linguistic Programming* – commonly abbreviated as NLP, but not to be mistaken for *Natural Language Processing* which deals with interactions between humans and computers – is a popular method of applying practices to read and influence people's behavior – your own, and other's. It was first introduced by American psychologist Richard Bandler (1950) and American linguist John Grinder (1940) in the 1970s as a new form of *psychotherapy* and nowadays its principles are widely used in various settings, mostly in business environments.

The basic idea is that Bandler and Grinder have, what they call "modeled" the best practices of some well-known psychologists and therapists of those days into a mixture of tools and techniques that can be used to steer oneself – or fellow human beings – to achieve certain goals. By "modeling" they meant that they described *how* something works, without any statements regarding *why* it might work that way.

The premise of the tools and techniques used is that there is a *supposed* connection between *neurological* processes, *language*, and behavior formed by experience (the *programming*). Over the years, NLP has been used by so many different therapists, practitioners, advocates, promoters, et cetera, that the scope of its use has become enormous. Anything that humans *experience* is a legitimate playing field, according to NLP advocates. This premise in itself should make your eyebrows lift, to say the least. Even though this quite astonishing omnipotent claim has resulted in a wide variety of tools and techniques and sub-branches of NLP, there are some common principles of NLP, often referred to as the "presuppositions of NLP". Below are some of the most well-known and applied principles, many of which can be found being adhered to regularly throughout organizations worldwide – also by people without any apparent knowledge of NLP itself.

- "The *map* is not the *territory*" – the principle that indicates that people subjectively observe reality, thus creating their own view (the *map*) of reality (the *territory*). NLP coaches then go to work with the *map*, not the reality.

- "Life and mind are *systemic processes*" – people and their relations are complex systems and processes. These systems and processes influence one another and create complex non-linear behavior. Thus, it's always good to look at descriptions of situations from different angles, which can be quite different, but equally valid. For instance, a problem in your team might look entirely different from your or your managers perspective. This is also believed to be true for one person – you can always look at a situation from different angles.
- "Every behavior is the result of *positive intention*" – NLP assumes that the behavior someone displays is the *best choice* that person could think of (perhaps even subconsciously). NLP coaches try to present *alternative choices* to help someone change *unwanted behavior*. Some NLP advocates even argue that *mental illness* is just an understandable choice, given the impossible pressure that society and family life put on individuals.
- "Rapport" – the *subjective* quality of a relationship with regards to *trust* and a *sense of ease*. Research into the effectiveness of traditional psychotherapy has already shown that the relationship between therapist and client

is crucial to the success of the therapy. NLP adds to this by focusing on what rapport exactly is, and what constitutes *good* rapport, and what *poor* rapport.

- "Choice versus Stuckness" – a large part of NLP is recognizing *stuckness*, and then helping the client see where there are more choices to get out of being stuck. "One option is no choice, two options is a dilemma, three or more options is a *choice*," is a much-used phrase you might have heard before.
- "The recipient determines the meaning of your communication" – your recipient might not understand what you meant to get across, but that's still the only thing that really counts. Once you grasp this, you will adjust your communication to get your opinion across the way you want it to land.
- "People have all the resources they need to succeed" – NLP coaches believe this to be helpful when attempting to make a change.
- "Different perspectives develop new choices" – because someone *in* a certain situation will see evolving events differently from someone *outside* that same situation, NLP considers it useful to move between *perceptual positions* in order to look at the situation from new angles and perhaps with less emotional involvement, to find new choices to escape the *stuckness*.

- "The structure of a problem matters most" – if two problems share the same structure, they can most likely be solved in similar ways. So, if you know how to solve one issue, apply the same path to the other issue which seemingly shares the same structure.
- "If what you're doing isn't working, try something else" – speaks for itself.
- "Use whatever works" – this principle, also known as *utilization*, says that if something works, it is to be considered useful.
- "Resistance to change results from unconscious unmet needs" – if a client resists changing, that is because they have other – unconscious – needs that need attention first. Only a skilled therapist can find and attend to those needs.
- "Body and mind interact" – the body and the mind of a person have a significant influence on each other. The way you stand, walk, breathe, sit, all impact your emotional state.
- "Only sensory observation counts as evidence" – only that which you are able to observe through the five senses is acceptable as evidence of patterns or structures. Speculation, hypothesis, and logic are useful, but those must always be tested through obtaining sensory evidence.
- "NLP is the study of personal subjective reality" – since everyone is different and experiences

situations in their own way – *idiosyncratic* – and since situations are themselves complex, NLP applies a *heuristic* and *iterative* approach, whereby the practitioner tries different approaches, observes feedback, forms hypotheses, and tests those with the client. Some say 90% of this process is information gathering and 10% is change work – and even that divide is considered artificial since the change work happens during the iterative process and is thus hard to separate from the rest.

- "Do not assume patterns to be universal" – because experiences are highly personal, any patterns you might find are assumed to be highly personal as well, unique to the client's life. If there are universal patterns, they aren't yet known, so you might as well ignore that idea and focus on the individual. NLP applies this motto to its own models as well – the practitioner should never assume models to apply to their client, but should always test and confirm.

- "There is no failure, only feedback" – since NLP implies a repetitive *trial and error* approach, failure is seen as feedback on what doesn't work. No worries, learn from the feedback, and onwards to the next iteration to

> learn some more. Failure is only truly a failure if you neglect to learn from it.

- "NLP works with self-perceived problems only" – instead of the therapist making a judgment call on what the problem of the client is, in NLP the client comes forward with a self-perceived problem they want to work on. Consequently, it is only the client who is to judge if the trajectory has worked or not.

Well, there you have it, the NLP *presuppositions* in a nutshell. Of course, there is much more to NLP than just this short list with limited explanations, but I hope it gives you an idea of the gist of it. You will probably recognize many of these principles from your work – especially if you work at an organization that adheres to Agile principles. Besides familiarity, the principles will most likely also invoke thoughts of appreciation. It all sounds pretty darn sensible, doesn't it? And that's exactly where the problems linger – our common sense is not always as right as we think it is, as we will see over and over again in the next chapters.

The fact that many of NLP's presuppositions *sound* pretty reasonable shouldn't blind you from what has actually been *proven* to be true. Between the early days of NLP and now, *all* of the underlying theories have been discarded by numerous studies around the world. Scientific reviews state that NLP is based on *outdated* metaphors of how the brain works and that it contains numerous factual *errors*. There is *no* scientific evidence supporting the claims made by NLP advocates and it has been discredited as *pseudoscience* by scientists worldwide. As a result, NLP is no longer widely used by psychotherapists (even though some do still use elements of it). The problem is, that all of this has somehow *not* stopped its adoption in the world of *business*. NLP is still being spread around in organizations worldwide. There are plenty of popular coaches, courses, and numerous schools of thought which are more or less based on NLP.

What to make of this then? Are all those NLP coaches dumb? Or, are they all unscrupulous con artists? I think not, in neither case. I've met quite a few NLP coaches in many organizations (I told you it was popular), and by far most of them are nice people with a genuine interest in psychology, coaching, and basically helping people become better versions of themselves. Looking at the evidence, however, I must conclude what I said in the previous paragraph, that NLP is a *pseudoscience*, with no proven evidence backing up its claims nor practices, no matter how nice it all seems. Just because there are plenty of *anecdotal success stories* doesn't mean NLP is the *reason* for those successes. Nor does it mean that other people's path to success is *your* path to success – even NLP itself claims that caveat. And even though NLP warns about not assuming patterns to be universal, NLP advocates just can't seem to be able to help themselves quoting successful people and telling their success stories. Most importantly, as with the aforementioned *growth mindset*, you should not be fooled into thinking that success (however you define it) is only a matter of *choice* and *effort*. We will see a lot of evidence to the contrary in the next chapter. To lift but a corner of the veil, much of what we *are* is defined by what we are *born* with – intelligence, personality, memory capacity, and – not to forget – our circumstances, like where we were born and where we grew up, and the societal system that was in place there.

The strange fact that a lack of scientific evidence does not seem to hold back the success of NLP is partly because of the great marketing apparatus behind many NLP coaches, but surely also in part because of *wishful thinking* that lives inside many organizations. Success stories do well with many people – our social media thrive because of that. How great is it then to hear of the successes of others that lie within *your* grasp, if only you would just step up to the plate and find the courage to swing, then surely you will hit a homerun too! Personally, I find it very strange that organizations put their eggs in this basket. They spend millions on coaches, sessions, and seminars, without any guarantee of success whatsoever. By stating that everyone already has what it takes to succeed, NLP slyly shifts the responsibility for succeeding to the client. If I were sick and I'd go the doctor and they'd tell me, "I have a great cutting-edge medicine here, but, if it works is all up to *you*", would you take it? What if they would add this: "we gave it to Sam and Sam is now the healthiest person in town! We also gave it to the Mayor of your city and your Mayor has recently been awarded 'Mayor of the Year'! Wow! That's great, isn't it? Surely you would want this great medicine for yourself as well!" Would you take it now? At some point you might wonder, well, *no harm, no foul*, right? What could go wrong? I might as well try it, and maybe, just maybe, I'm the lucky one for whom it *does* do wonders! No hurt in trying! Well, that's not completely true either. There are examples of NLP coaching trajectories gone horribly awry, like, for instance, with a group of NLP coaches in Wales that were trying to help veterans with their *Post-Traumatic Stress Disorder* as part of a program funded by charity. After three days of therapy by the NLP coaches, the veterans felt worse than before, with some even feeling *suicidal*. Apart from extreme experiences like these, it doesn't seem healthy to rely on something that *might* possibly do something for you – it leaves too much room for error or waste. I have no doubt that most people feel pretty good right after an NLP coaching session, but who is checking up on them after three weeks? No research has either been done, or has shown, that NLP coaching has lasting positive results. From the success stories that are being told, it is not proven – or even tested – that they are the *result* of NLP.

Long story short, I'd put my time and money someplace else – stick with science, trust what has been proven and replicated numerous times, you can't go wrong with that.

Thinking yourself out of a depression

One of the common themes between NLP and NLP-derived methods – like for instance the work of famous motivational coach Tony Robbins – is the presumption that people who suffer from depression got themselves in their depression by thinking in a particular way – a *wrong* way – and that they should be able to *think* themselves out of their depression as well – of course with the help from the (NLP) therapist who knows exactly how to do that.

Robbins, in multiple of his performances that you can find on the internet, chides renowned comedian and actor Robin Williams, who died of suicide invoked by his lifelong depression, for being a *total failure*. The reasoning of Robbins is that success without fulfillment is the ultimate failure, and the fault of the failure lies within the thinking of the person. How one chooses to think about the circumstances that the person may find themselves in, is the pinnacle of the matter, according to Robbins. He adds to that, "fulfillment is not a science, it's art."

The real danger in this line of reasoning is that the fault is put in the court of the depressed, while psychologists and therapists worldwide nowadays fully acknowledge that depression is a serious medical *illness*. Like you would never even dare think about blaming a quadriplegic for not standing up and walking about, you should never blame someone who is depressed for feeling gloomy. It is a clear-cut case of *victim-blaming* which yields unknown and potentially catastrophic results for the blamed, the depressed.

Motivational coaches – of which there never seems to be a shortage of – are very good at playing into our aspirations for success. They present many anecdotes of success stories as if they were recipes for us to use to achieve our own goals. If you fail, you are left with the feeling that you failed to follow the recipe. You didn't put in the hard work, the recipe was good – look at what it did for all those successful people! However, if all the people in the world who ever read a self-help book or attended a motivational seminar had become a millionaire, the world would be flooded with them, but alas. Don't fall into the trap of self-blaming. The success stories are personal, filled with having luck, and certainly not generally applicable. Most people – NLP fans or not – struggle through life just like you and me, there are no shortcuts.

Toxic positivity

One of the hallmarks of today's coaching is the ever-present *positivity*. Some of that can be traced back to NLP – think of, "there is no failure, only feedback".

We all have an inner mood *baseline*. We will be happier at times, sadder at others, but in general, we return to a certain baseline level. The baseline level will differ from person to person. Some are more inclined to be gloomy while others always see the positive side of things. Besides the energy-draining efforts to pull someone from their baseline, it also doesn't make sense to always try and be positive. As *grief* experts tell us, it's important for us to acknowledge loss or failure. It's important to not force yourself away from the pain you actually feel deep inside. If you try, your true emotions will simmer unconsciously and after a while, you will feel *exhausted*. The unattended pain of loss or failure might turn into long-lasting *suffering*. Pain is inevitable but suffering is optional. Instead, acknowledging and exploring your pain will eventually lead you back to your baseline. You don't need to do this all by yourself, you can always consult a qualified therapist to help you return to an acceptable baseline.

Forced positivity is not the solution to deal with loss or failure, but what *does* help in dealing with pain is realizing how resilient you are and being optimistic about recovery.

So, the next time your team fails to meet a deadline, or when your team has caused a major failure for the organization, don't try to overcompensate by waving away the troubles and being overly positive about the situation. It's okay to let the pain sink in. Talk about the failure within the team and let people share their emotions. Attend to the pain *now* to avoid suffering in the long run. Just as an individual will always return to a baseline, so will a team.

Endnote on the myths

There are real dangers hidden in adopting non-scientifically proven methods, so why not play it safe and look at what is actually supported by the vast and scrupulous world of science? Let me assure you that the scientifically proven facts are no less fascinating than the *clickbait* you encounter daily on your social media news feeds. Moreover, with the scientific evidence in your corner, you have a more profound basis upon which to build your effective behavior in the modern workplace.

Chapter Two – The Self

Now that we've seen what doesn't really work, it's time to dive into the psychology that *does* work in our workplace. We'll start closest to home and as small as possible – with ourselves. Or perhaps I should say, our *self*. What actually is *the self*?

The Astonishing Hypothesis

Philosopher René Descartes (1596-1650) posed in his *dualistic* view that we consist of both a *body* and a separate *mind*. The self, in his view, is the mind that thinks. In his 1994 book *The Astonishing Hypothesis*, British scientist Francis Crick (1916-2004) – who jointly won a Nobel Prize in 1962 for co-discovering the double helix structure of DNA – proposed what many scholars nowadays maintain, namely that without the physical brain, there is no mind, and therefore, no self. This would – as a side note – take away the possibilities of an afterlife or reincarnation. The mind and the self would cease to exist if the body died. I could fill a cabinet with writings and discussions on this topic alone.

The Mind and Free Will

However controversial the last statement might already seem to many, some modern thinkers take things a step further still. American philosopher and neuroscientist Sam Harris (1967), for instance, submits that which seems to be the most notable – if not the most important – aspect of the self, namely *free will*, is an *illusion*. He claims that everything we think and do is actually predetermined by both our genes and the circumstances which formed our lives right up to the moment when we think we make a conscious decision. Harris poses we don't really make conscious decisions. Do you know exactly the moment when you make a decision? If you have to choose between A and B, and you finally decide upon B, why is that? Where did the decision to pick B come from? Scientists like Harris propound that the thought seemingly comes from nowhere, but that brain scans show activity slightly before the tested individual indicates that a decision was made, which thus adds to the point that even our thoughts are predetermined. Whatever social implications that theory might actually hold is food for thought, but not for now. If we at least agree on the self being our conscious self, our true person, then we can discuss *personality*.

Personality

If we consider our style of behavior to be fairly consistent across time and space, we can define *personality* as the relatively consistent patterns of thought, feeling, and behavior that characterize each person as a unique individual. Thus, *personality* refers to a person's general style of interacting with the world, especially with other people.

The uniqueness of individuals encourages an innate fascination with *differences* between individuals. Noticing, and indeed focusing, on such differences helps us in everyday life with making decisions about how to deal with the people around us. Whom to trust, whom to care for, whose advice to ignore, whom we want as friends, or even as a partner.

The central concept in personality psychology is the *trait*. Traits are an integral part of a person. How the traits will manifest as *behavior* depends on triggers the individual perceives from the current environment. Different environments might trigger different behaviors based on the same trait. Someone with a tendency towards aggressiveness might blow up in an environment that is safe for them, like the home environment, but might resort to passive-aggressive behavior in a work environment.

Traits

A trait is not a binary concept. One is not, for instance, totally aggressive or absolutely non-aggressive, but rather, it is a sliding scale, with most people being somewhere in the middle and with few exceptions on the outer ends. If you observe an aggressive person next to a kind person in the same environment, you will see that if the two receive the same triggers, the aggressive person will respond in an aggressive manner *sooner* than the kind person. It is by observing behavior that we derive the trait. We see someone argue and fight a lot and derive therefrom that the person is high in the trait aggressiveness.

One of the pioneers of personality psychology was American psychologist Gordon Allport (1897-1967), who – in 1937 – identified no less than 17,953 descriptors of personality, like "kind", "aggressive", "rude", "carefree", "trusting", et cetera. Many of the terms that Allport listed are overlapping and some are almost the same as others.

To make more practical use of trait descriptions, British American psychologist Raymond Cattell (1905-1998) condensed Allport's 17,953 adjectives down to 170 that he took to be distinct, and later on identified 16 basic traits out of those. He devised a questionnaire of nearly 200 statements about behavior to help measure the traits of people, such as, "I like to go to parties".

OCEAN – The Big Five

Many later trait researchers found even Cattell's 16 traits too overly complex and redundant. After many studies of people of all ages, in many different cultures, a general consensus has been agreed on in the world of psychology, which is now known as *the Big Five* theory, or the *five-factor model*, of personality. The acronym OCEAN can be used to remember the five traits applied to describe personality.

O stands for one's *Openness* to new experiences. Someone with a high openness seeks out new experiences, whereas someone with a low openness, or non-openness, is more conservative and prefers familiarity to novelty.

C is for *Conscientiousness*. Someone with high conscientiousness is able to control their own behavior in order to reach their goals. On the other end, someone with low conscientiousness will have a hard time keeping a schedule and be disorganized, and even be unreliable.

E stands for *Extraversion*. An extravert person prefers intense and frequent interpersonal interactions and receives energy from being around other people. Introvert people, on the other end, prefer a few close friends and don't mind, or even like, being alone. Being around other people sucks energy from them.

A is for *Agreeableness*. Someone who is agreeable regards others with sympathy and acts unselfishly, as opposed to someone who is not concerned with other people and tends to be antagonistic, and even hostile.

N stands for *Neuroticism*. Someone with high neuroticism experiences many forms of emotional distress, has unrealistic ideas and troublesome urges. On the other end, someone with low neuroticism is emotionally stable, doesn't get upset easily, and is not prone to depression.

Researchers have found that if you test a person on the Big Five traits whether they are in their twenties, their forties, or their sixties, they will score relatively stable on these traits. If you are an extravert at twenty-five, you are very likely to still be an extravert when you're sixty-five, and so on.

Intelligence

This brings us to another much-debated aspect of our self, *intelligence*. Intelligence is generally considered to be the capacity in *reasoning, solving problems,* and *acquiring new knowledge.* Psychologists have long had an interest in measuring intelligence, mostly from what they were asked to do by others, like school systems and employers. In 1905, French psychologist Alfred Binet (1857-1911) and his colleague Théodore Simon

(1873-1961) developed the Binet-Simon Intelligence Scale. Their method was based on the idea that intelligence is best described as a collection of various mental abilities that are loosely related to each other. Their test was used foremost to identify children who were not profiting enough from their schooling and might benefit from special attention. Therefore it focused explicitly on skills required for schoolwork, like memory, vocabulary, common knowledge, use of numbers, understanding of time, and the ability to combine ideas. The outcomes of the *Binet-Simon* test were held against the teachers' ratings of each child's classroom performance to improve on the validity of the test, even though this method in itself is not ideal, because the test was compared to that which it sought to improve upon. Nevertheless, by 1908, the Binet-Simon test was widely used in France, and not long after that, English translations became even more popular in England and North America.

IQ tests

In 1916, a modification of the Binet-Simon test was made at Stanford University and became commonly used and known in North America as the *Stanford-Binet Scale*, and is still in use today. Another variation of the Binet-Simon test was made by David Wechsler (1896-1981) in the 1930s, of which the offspring is widely used these days. The *Wechsler Adult*

Intelligence Scale, Fourth Edition, the *WAIS-IV* is such a scale. This test consists of four subtests in the areas of *verbal comprehension*, *perceptual processing*, *working memory*, and *processing speed*. The results of these subtests are combined into a person's *Intelligence Quotient* or *IQ* score. The results of large groups of people are compared. The person whose performance is exactly average for the comparison group is assigned an IQ score of 100. If you scored below average, you score an IQ lower than 100, and if you scored above average, you score an IQ higher than 100. The overall distribution of the IQ scores of such a large group matches the *bell-shaped curve* of what is known as a *normal distribution*. This results in about 68 percent of the people having IQ scores between 85 and 115, and 95 percent of the population having an IQ between 70 and 130. Less than 2.5 percent of the people score below 70, and, equally, less than 2.5 percent score above 130.

The question, of course, is, what does it all mean? What does it say, when you have an IQ of 137? Does that mean guaranteed success in life? Or does it only tell you that you're very good at taking tests, or worse, proficient at taking IQ tests? Much research has been done over the years into the correlation between IQ scores and achievements in real life, and the overwhelming evidence states that there is indeed a significant relationship between a high IQ score and overall good performance in life. When measuring performance at work, done by supervisors, colleagues and researchers, it turns out that for jobs that are highly mentally complex, IQ tests are actually better predictors of performance than any other measurement, even when compared to testing specific knowledge and skills related to the job.

For those of you that were looking for the politically correct opposite conclusion, alas, the evidence is very convincing. At the same time, evidence for such a relationship between *Emotional Intelligence*, or *EI*, and success in life, is far *less* apparent, however much that is in disagreement with widespread popular belief. Author and journalist Daniel Goleman (1946) wrote a bestseller called "Emotional Intelligence" in 1995, and proposed that *EI* matters twice as much as *IQ* when it comes to superior performance in leaders. Others in the scientific community, however, have found no significant relationship between *EI* markers and leadership performance, whereas general intelligence (*IQ*) correlated very closely with leadership.

Intelligence as a Good Predictor

Much study has gone into the relationship between intelligence and overall performance. Many have searched for an overarching concept that would provide an easy answer to the broad concept of intelligence.

Ask twenty researchers how they think of intelligence, and you'll get twenty different answers. Some ideas, however, have found more footing than others. Charles Spearman (1863-1945), who studied in Leipzig under Wilhelm Wundt – as we've seen, the first modern psychologist – posited the idea that if you test a person on many different aspects of intelligence, you will find a positive correlation between the results. So, if a person scores well on, for instance, a short-term memory test, that same person is likely to score well on a test of their vocabulary, or even on a test with visual puzzles. Spearman coined the term *g* to refer to a *general* underlying factor of intelligence. Next to *g*, he used *s* to refer to the *specific* factor of intelligence that was being tested in a particular test.

Raymond Cattell, who we saw earlier when discussing personality, and who was a student of Spearman, proposed to split *g* into two separate forms of intelligence, namely *fluid* and *crystallized* intelligence. With *fluid* intelligence, he meant the ability to identify differences and similarities between items that a person has *never seen before. Crystallized* intelligence, on the other hand, is derived directly from *experience.* The interesting part of this distinction is that the two kinds of intelligence evolve measurably differently over a lifespan. *Fluid* intelligence peaks in your early twenties and goes downhill from there, while *crystallized* intelligence is at its very best in your fifties, and doesn't diminish that much after that.

There also is a measurable linkage between *mental speed* and *g*. How faster one can inspect and respond during a test, how higher their *IQ* is likely to be. Which brings us to what are called *Executive Functions*. These basic information-processing mechanisms are *working memory*, *switching*, and *inhibition*.

The term *working memory* is related to mental speed, to the speed in which one can add or delete items from working memory. *Switching* refers to the ability to shift between different tasks or mindsets. And *inhibition* prevents you from losing focus, keeping out distractions.

I know we haven't discussed memory much yet, but all you need to know right now is that *working memory* is the memory that lasts only a few seconds, with which you consciously operate. If you don't pay attention to items in your working memory, they fade and drop from it. Also, the number of items you can hold in your working memory is very limited, the general idea being seven items, plus or minus two, depending on genetics and circumstances.

The ability to rapidly take items in and out of *working memory*, along with the ability to *switch* context quickly, and the ability to keep *focus*, helps to increase your *general intelligence*.

Heritability

Another interesting aspect of intelligence is the fact that we are all born with different levels of it. That sounds like an open door, but where intelligence comes from has been at the center of much debate throughout the years. This terrain is what we call the *nature versus nurture debate.* Is intelligence determined more by genes or more by environment? Another, more precise, way of putting it is, are the differences we see in intelligence between individuals more the result of the differences between their genes, or more the result of the differences between their environments? This discussion turns out to be without end, since the two dimensions are inseparable. If you compare two people who grew up in very different environments, it makes sense that any differences in intelligence have to do with the differences between the environments. If you compare two people who grew up in exactly the same environment, logic dictates that any differences in intelligence are related to the differences between their genes.

Hereto, the concept of *heritability* comes into play. Heritability is the degree to which variation in a particular trait, like intelligence, within a particular population of individuals, stems from genetic differences as opposed to environmental differences. Heritability is often quantified by a number ranging from 0 to 1, called the *heritability coefficient.* When it is 0, *none* of the differences in a trait are related to inheritance, and when it is 1, *all* of the differences in a trait are related to inheritance.

Studies of heritability often include tests with twins. For instance, if your hypothesis is, that intelligence is highly heritable, you would expect monozygotic twins who grew up together in the same household to have almost the same *IQ*. Numerous studies with twins have shown this to be the case indeed. The strange conclusion attached to this high heritability is that the environment in which one grows up is of less importance to intelligence in later life, which would render much of many parent's efforts to create the perfect study circumstances for their offspring rather useless. Tests show that monozygotic twins who grew up apart from each other show a more correlated intelligence even than dizygotic twins who grew up together.

It must be said, however, that the genetic effect on intelligence has been found to have a much greater effect when the parents were highly educated. So, if the parents have low education, the environment plays a much bigger role in determining the intelligence of the individual. This has been explained by the idea that "harmful" environments, in this case, low education, have more impact on the development of traits than average or above-average environments. The transient nature of the effect of family on IQ is perhaps the most surprising result that has emerged from studies of IQ correlations.

Not surprisingly, taking into account the results of general intelligence testing, the *Executive Functions* – working memory, switching, and inhibition – are also mostly heritable, as is *mental speed*. Research has further shown that *fluid* and *crystallized intelligence* are both about equally heritable.

The concept of heritability does not answer one big question, however, and that is, can you *grow* intelligence? And if so, can you grow intelligence during all of your life, or just when you're a kid?

Where Binet designed his *IQ* tests specifically to determine which schoolchildren did not fully benefit from the way of teaching, thus implicitly believing that *IQ* could be raised for all by using properly adjusted personal teachings, Spearman maintained *g* is something you are born with.

Psychologists today agree that, yes, you can foster your intelligence through active, intellectual engagement with the world. It helps therefore to have a personality that is high in openness. If you're curious, independent of mind, and have broad interests, you are likely to choose a lifestyle that will raise your intelligence, even throughout your lifetime, bearing in mind that *fluid* intelligence drops over time and *crystallized* intelligence can rise even well into your fifties or even further. The question remains, just how much can you grow your intelligence and other abilities?

Memory

Before traveling from *intelligence* to the associated *reasoning*, I'll have to explain a few other phenomena of interest. First, there is *memory*. You might think our memory is like our internal "hard disk", analogous to a computer's hard drive, but it's not as simple as that. As might know, your computer has two kinds of memories, the hard drive – or these days, the flash drive – and a few computer chips which provide the RAM, the *Random Access Memory*, also known as "working memory". That is actually closer to how our own memory works.

To paint the full picture, we start with *sensory input*, information your brain retrieves from your senses – vision, smell, sound, touch, and taste. Your senses actually have a memory with a very, very short lifespan. You can check this sort of memory yourself quite easily. For instance, when you look at a bright light first and then turn it off, you will – for a short period of time – still see the bright light.

Another great example is the following regarding memory of sound. You have no doubt had a friend talk to you while you weren't really listening. When they noticed and asked you, "what did I just say?", you probably have been able to quote their last sentence verbatim, leaving them stunned and without an argument. That was your *sensory memory* at work. If your friend would have been cunning enough to ask you what their story was *actually* about, you wouldn't have gotten off the hook so easily.

If you do pay *attention* to your sensory memory, the information goes into your *short-term memory* or *working memory*. Mind you, however, that if you don't *rehearse* the information in your *working memory*, it is quickly lost. To be able to remember things on a longer term, you need a process called *encoding* to store the information in your *long-term memory*. Through a process called *retrieval*, you can obtain information from your *long-term memory* back into your *working memory* again – even though some information may be lost over time. You might remember – no pun intended – that *working memory* is part of the *Executive Functions* (the other two are *switching* and *inhibition*), which contribute a great deal to the *general intelligence* of an individual.

The reason we need *attention* is that the senses produce a lot of information, which we can't all keep in our working memory. As a matter of fact, the short-term memory has such a limited capacity that it can only hold about *seven plus or minus two* items, depending on the person and their circumstances. This is referred to as *Miller's law*, after psychologist George

A. Miller, who – in 1956 – wrote his paper, "The Magical Number Seven, Plus or Minus Two: Some Limits on Our Capacity for Processing Information". It's important to notice that the "items" that can be held in the short-term store, are more like *chunks* of memory, rather than single items. The way to think about this, is this – it's not like you can retain only seven digits in your memory, like, say, "1, 3, 7, 2, 4, 5, 9", but actually more like, "132, 454, 764, 385, 497, 625, 267", or better yet, "I have to buy lettuce at the grocery store, go to the dentist in the afternoon, take the car through the carwash, get the kids to the hairdresser, buy aspirin at the drugstore, fill the car up at the gas station, and buy a gift for my nephew at the toy store" – I think you probably catch the drift here. The point is that the actual *nature* of the content of a chunk is not very limited, even though a chunk is just that, one single piece of information.

Those of you familiar with the aforementioned *Scrum framework* will no doubt feel a tingling of recognition in *Miller's law*. In the original *Scrum Guide,* it used to say that the optimal team size was *seven plus or minus two* team members. In later versions – including the current one – a size between three and nine team members is recommended. The idea behind the limited number of team members evolved from the idea that it would be too hard to keep track of what is going on in your team if there were more than seven plus two members in your team.

Personally, I think the link between *Miller's law* and the ideal number of team members is far-fetched. Our short-term store has a very short life span. If you no longer think about the chunks, they disappear within *seconds*. Thus, short-term memory would not be a valid reason to limit the size of a team. Moreover, I think we already know that without perhaps thinking about it explicitly. How big is a soccer team? Eleven people. How big is a squad in the army? Generally between eight and fourteen soldiers. Et cetera. And do those constructions fail because the team members find that their working memory hinders them in cooperation with their fellow team members? "Who the heck is that on the other side of the field and what on Earth are they doing there?" I don't think so. Your familiarization with fellow team members and their work has much more to do with your long-term memory.

The *encoding* that is done when information is stored in the long-term memory, can be deliberate – for instance, when you're studying. When you try to memorize words, or countries and their capitals, or historical dates, then you are consciously encoding information in your long-term memory, but most of the encoding actually happens unnoticed. When you are interested in certain information, your brain starts to encode all by itself. If you're interested in comic books, the encoding will make sure you recognize Wonder Woman in two weeks' time, when you see a poster for a movie about Wonder Woman. You didn't deliberately sit down and focus heavily on memorizing what she looks like, the processes in your brain did that automatically.

To be able to recognize Wonder Woman on the movie poster, you need another process, called *retrieval*, that controls the flow of information from your long-term memory into your short-term store. Again, this can be very deliberate, when you actively try to remember something, but mostly it happens quite automatically. You see the poster and you just know it's Wonder Woman on it.

Memory is further split into *explicit* and *implicit* memory. *Explicit* – or *declarative* – memory is what you access when asked specifically to remember something, for instance for reflection, planning, or problem-solving. *Implicit* memory is the nonverbal and unconscious memory that you use frequently and automatically. Take, for instance, the memory needed to be able to ride a bicycle, or pick up a glass to drink.

Explicit memory is further split between *episodic* and *semantic* memory – where episodic memory refers to one's own past experiences, and semantic memory relates to the general knowledge of the world, including the meaning of words (literally *semantics*).

Learning

Of great interest to people in a modern workplace, is how to learn new things. These days, we are all constantly learning new skills. If you're not learning, you're standing still – and if you're standing still, you're falling behind. How then, can you learn new things as quickly as possible and keep them in your memory? This question is also very relevant to people who teach or coach others.

What you basically want, is for information to go from sensory input, through the working memory, into the long-term memory – and then be retrievable at will. We already saw that you need *attention* to get information from sensory input into working memory, and a process called *encoding* to get it into the long-term memory. What helps the *encoding* is what psychologists call *elaboration* or *elaborative rehearsal* – mainly *deep thinking* about the information. Deep thinking entails more than just repeating the information in your head. Elaboration is more about *understanding* information than *memorizing* it, and as it turns out, understanding information is the key to remembering information best. Thus, the approach of modern teaching is to make sure students *understand* the information, rather than simply being able to *recall* it.

A few interesting tricks to finish up this sidestep into memory. First, *organizing* the information (hierarchically) helps to remember it better. If you can't find any natural organization in the information, make it up. For instance, if you have to remember a string of random letters, create a sentence out of them by using the random letters as first letters of the words that form your sentence.

Furthermore, *visualization* helps the encoding process. Studies have shown that the part of the brain that is concerned with spatial understanding – the hippocampus – is also involved in encoding and retrieval of information to and from long-term memory. You can make good use of that by imagining storing information in a three-dimensional place – for instance in your own house. You'll remember it better if you put the first principle of the Agile Manifesto under your bed – as an exercise in your mind.

One last "trick", which is more like sound advice. If you study first and then go to sleep for the night, you'll remember the information much better the next day. So instead of studying through the night before an exam, you'd be better off studying during the day and getting a good night's rest after that.

A final word of caution on memory. As it turns out, long-term memory is not stored and retrieved "as is". Instead, when it is retrieved, it is *modified* with the latest information. This process gives rise to the possibility of false memories. You might think you remember some event quite exactly but in reality, your earlier memories could have been partly overwritten by later experiences, or even suggestions. On the other hand, studies show that retrieval might also strengthen the memory further, depending on what happens with the information once retrieved. Learning new information, these studies show, works best if you retrieve the information often and affirm the retrieved information again.

Slow and Fast Thinking

In his famous 2011 best-seller, *Thinking, Fast and Slow*, Israeli-American cognitive psychologist Daniel Kahneman (1934) explains that we basically think in two distinct fashions: *system one* is fast, instinctive, and emotional, while *system two* is slower, more deliberative, and more logical. For most of the day, *system one* thinking will suffice. When you're making a cup of coffee, you do that without too much thought – you can most probably do it while having a conversation with someone. But, when you're trying out a new recipe for dinner, you need to stop doing anything else and really focus on the job at hand – you need *system two* thinking.

Another way of saying it is, *system one* thinking happens *unconsciously* and *system two* thinking is *conscious* thinking.

Consciousness

This brings us to *consciousness* – or rather, *self-consciousness* – a much-debated term throughout the history of both psychology and philosophy. In his 1996 book *The Conscious Mind*, Australian philosopher David Chalmers (1966) describes what he calls the *easy* problems of consciousness – like being able to explain how the brain physically works – versus the *hard problem* of explaining why we feel anything at all at any given time. What is the use of *feeling*?

These days, many psychologists define *consciousness* in a very practical sense, as the experience of one's own mental events in such a manner that one can report on them to others. The practicality lies in the idea that you can ask a person to relate their thoughts, and therefore check their *consciousness* or *awareness*.

Another way to approach consciousness is by looking at *attention*. We've already discussed the way attention influences how information flows from sensory memory to the short-term store or working memory. Once information is inside the working memory, we *consciously* work with it.

Alan Baddeley (1934) developed the most influential model of working memory, dividing it into three interacting components – the *phonological loop*, the *visuospatial sketchpad*, and the *central executive*.

Later on, Baddeley introduced a fourth component, the *episodic buffer*.

The phonological loop is what we consciously use to keep information in our working memory. If someone tells you their telephone number, you probably keep repeating the number in your mind until you've typed it into your mobile as a new entry – that's the phonological loop at work. The interesting thing is that the faster you can speak to yourself, the more information you can retain in your working memory. Generally, people can subvocally keep in working memory about as much verbal material as they can state aloud in two seconds (Baddeley). People who speak fast out loud, tend to be able to speak fast in their conscious mind and are therefore able to keep more information in their short-term memory. Also, language matters. If your language uses long words or elaborate sentences to describe things, your working memory will be more limited than for someone who uses a very succinct language. For instance, in Chinese, the numbers one to ten are all single-syllable words, which makes it easier for Chinese speaking people to remember larger amounts of numbers.

What's even more interesting, is that what is called the *working-memory span* – the ability to perform some "work" with a number of items in working memory – gives a good indication of cognitive abilities. In other words, the more items you are able to work with, in your *consciousness*, the more proficient you most probably are in higher-level abilities like reading, writing, mathematics, et cetera.

Reasoning

If we use our memories to deal adaptively with the present and the future, we are *reasoning*. A large part of what we call *intelligence* is our capacity to *reason*. We are able to reason in different ways. We can use *analogies* and *induction*, or we can use *deduction* and *insight*. More about this in the following paragraphs.

Analogies

Similarities between occurring events and what we have memorized from the past help us think about future events. If we see dark clouds gathering and the wind is picking up, we know from past experience that rain is likely to fall pretty soon. If we see an object that has keys with symbols on them, we know from similarities with keyboards we've seen in the past, that we can most probably type in some information to interact. The ability to recognize similarities defines a large portion of our capacity to reason.

Psychologists use the term *analogy* slightly differently from everyday use, in a sense that the similarity should not be that obvious. For instance, a sneaker and a boot are *not* considered by psychologists to fall under the category *analogous*, for they are *too* similar. But they do find an analogy between a sneaker and a car tire, since both share the similar function of touching the ground and giving grip for better and more comfortable movement, even though their physical appearance is quite different.

In reasoning, analogies appear in formats like "A is to B as X is to Y". So, following our example above, "*sneaker* is to *human* as *tire* is to *car*". It speaks for itself that the more life experience you have, the easier it is to find analogies from your memory.

In so-called *Raven's Progressive Matrices* tests – which are part of IQ tests – images are used instead of words, so as to eliminate the possibility of misunderstanding certain words, or perhaps not even knowing them. This makes these very reliable tests about reasoning, which in place makes them very reliable tests of intelligence.

Using analogies can be very useful to be able to understand difficult problems. Describing an analogous yet simpler version of a problem will help others comprehend the more difficult counterpart in the analogy.

Raven's Progressive Matrices test

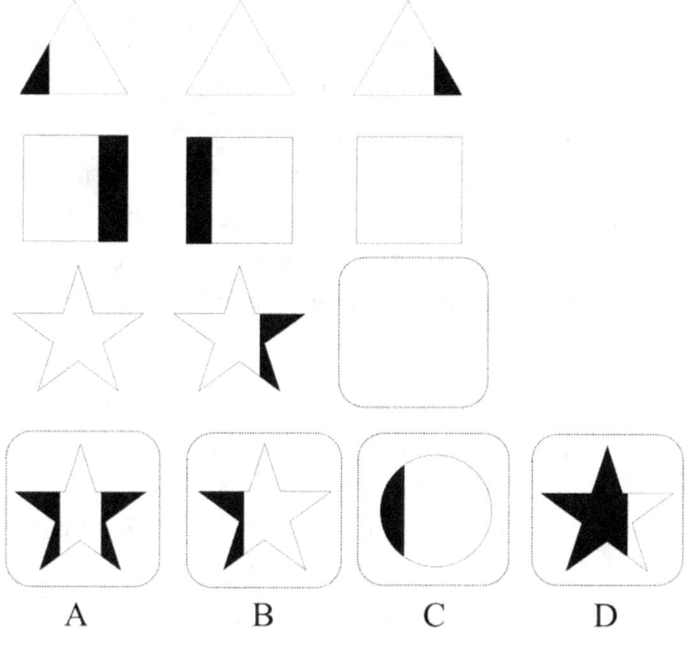

Even though analogies can be very enlightening, you do need extensive knowledge about the concepts that are being compared to be able to understand the analogy. An analogy that might work in one environment, might totally misfire in another. Understanding your audience is key here.

Research with modern brain scans – so-called fMRI's – has taught us that we use quite a bit of our brain to make analogies. To be more precise, we use multiple areas of our *prefrontal cortex*, the front end of our brain that is more heavily evolved than in any other species we know.

Cognitive neuroscientist Michael Vendetti and his colleagues have found that we are actually *not* very good at using analogies to solve *new* problems we face, but that *practice* makes us better at it. Since the use of analogies can be very helpful in understanding difficult issues, *practicing* making analogies is a wise choice. Vendetti and colleagues suggest the following to promote the use of analogies:

1. Provide opportunities for people to make connections between new and previously learned concepts.
2. Present the simpler and the more difficult parts of an analogy simultaneously.
3. Provide additional cues, such as gestures, to highlight the similarities.
4. Highlight the differences as well, and explicitly indicate if, and where, the analogy goes wrong.
5. Use relational language to emphasize shared relations.

Inductive Reasoning

We can use the experiences we've had and the observations we've made to draw general conclusions about something. We can even use other people's experiences and observations that – together with our own – provide *some* evidence for a (seemingly) general truth. This method of reasoning is called *inductive reasoning*. The problem with this type of reasoning is that the conclusion you reach might *not* be true at all.

For instance, if you've had a bad experience with the IT-helpdesk of your organization, and your closest colleague has had a similar bad experience, it would be easy for you to induce from both your experiences that the helpdesk really sucks. Little do you know that the same helpdesk provides adequate help to dozens of other colleagues every single day – you and your colleague just happened to be the odd ones out.

Inductive reasoning is particularly vulnerable to *biases* of all sorts.

Heuristics and Biases

I've mentioned Daniel Kahneman a few paragraphs back when discussing *Thinking Fast and Slow*. In 2002, this cognitive psychologist won the *Nobel Memorial Prize in Economic Sciences* for the work on *decision-making* he and his colleague Amos Tversky (1937-1996) did. Tversky and Kahneman developed their *prospect theory* which established a cognitive basis for common errors that arise from *heuristics* and *biases*. *Heuristics* are rules of thumb – simple strategies that can be used to quickly find solutions to complex problems – for instance, by focusing on the most relevant aspects of a problem. Heuristic processes are used to find solutions *most likely to be correct* – which does not mean, however, that heuristics are always right.

What Kahneman and Tversky found was that *cognitive biases* influence especially the faster thinking, the *system one* thinking. "Jumping to conclusions," is a very apt phrase in this respect.

The Availability Bias

If we continue the helpdesk example, then we see that our conclusion about the helpdesk's quality was based upon our very limited set of two people's experiences. We could have asked a few more colleagues perhaps, but still, our set would be limited in availability. Too limited actually to draw a proper conclusion from. We thereby evolve a bias against our helpdesk because of the limited availability of data. In this case, we know very well that we have many more colleagues that might have different experiences with the helpdesk, but we would probably find it too much of a hassle to go and ask all of their opinions. It's far easier – and faster – to form an opinion based on our own limited experience.

Tversky and Kahneman used a simple experiment to show the availability bias at work. They asked students if they thought the letter *d* would more likely be the first letter of a word, or more likely be the third letter of a word. Before reading on, what do you think?

While most people thought you'd find the *d* as the first letter of a word more often, the actual correct answer is that the *d* is more likely to be the third letter. Of course, people find it much harder to think of a word in which the *d* is the third letter than to think of words that start with a *d*.

While we may find these two examples not too distressing – and maybe even funny – there are occasions in which the availability bias has far more severe consequences. For instance, when the press tends to report on crime committed by black people disproportionately more than on crime committed by white people, society at large grows a bias that provides its members with plenty more examples of crime committed by black people to remember than of crime committed by white people. Research has shown that the press actually disinforms us in this exact disproportionate manner. This form of the availability bias actually fuels the institutional racism in our Western societies, which is a very real and pressing problem, especially if your skin happens to be black.

The Confirmation Bias

Another common bias is the confirmation bias, which emphasizes what we already believe. If you have somehow come to think that men are better at IT than women, you will find examples in your environment that confirm that belief. Examples to the contrary are easily dismissed or even overlooked.

A more abstract example can be found in an experiment that Peter Wason did in 1960. He asked people to guess the rule that he had made up for a sequence of numbers. For instance, he said, 4, 6, 8. The participants were then given the opportunity to respond with their own sequence of numbers and ask him if the sequence followed his rule, to which he would reply only with a yes or a no. What was striking was that people are inclined to come up with similar sequences as Wason gave them to begin with, only to confirm their hunches. So they would for instance reply with 10, 12, 14, which Wason confirmed abided by his made-up rule. In the end, participants would confidently claim that the rule would be to add 2 to each consecutive number, while in reality, the rule Wason made up was as simple as any increasing sequence of numbers.

The trick to get around your own assumptions that only reinforce what you already thought, is to ask questions that would deny your assumptions if true. So, if you ask if 1, 2, 3 follows the rule, then you know adding 2 is not part of the rule. And if you ask 8, 6, 4 and 4, 8, 6 then you find out that the numbers do need to go up.

In other interesting experiments, which relate more to what we encounter in our work environments, some participants were asked to interview someone they didn't know to find out if that person was an introvert. Other participants were asked to find out if the person was an extravert. Typically, the participants would ask questions that would reinforce the assumed demeanor of the interviewee. Supposed extraverts were asked questions like, "do you like to go out?", and supposed introverts were asked questions like, "are you shy when you meet new people?" Given the tendency to respond mostly with yes to interview questions like these, the confirmation bias only strengthened the assumptions, no matter what the assumption was.

The interesting thing to note is that confirmation bias is not related to intelligence. No matter how smart you are, we all fall into this trap if we don't watch out. A good thing to keep in mind in meetings in your organization. Are we asking the right questions? Are we asking 10, 12, 14, or are we asking 8, 6, 4, and 4, 8, 6?

As you might imagine, the combination of the availability bias and the confirmation bias can be a deadly poison that reinforces itself. If you see the news and come to believe that black people are more prone to crime than white people, and with every other news story that belief is reinforced with more and more examples, then institutional racism is the consequence.

In an organization in transformation, it's easy for people who were against any form of change from the beginning to find examples that confirm their hesitations towards change. Providing transparent data on what's really happening in the organization is crucial, as well as keep asking the right questions.

The Predictable-World Bias

A somewhat different bias from the availability and confirmation biases is the predictable-world bias. We tend to overestimate the amount of order in the world around us, we see order where it does not exist. Many times, coincidence is just that, but we often fail to recognize it as such and opt to believe there is a reason. If you've held a great presentation at work one week and another successful one two weeks later, and you just happened to be wearing the same sock those two presentation days, they are likely to become your "lucky socks", even though your socks had nothing to do with the quality of your presentation.

Though most of us realize fully well that there is no such thing as luck, it's somehow hard to resist the idea. Imagine a die with two sides painted blue and four sides painted yellow. You will receive a dollar each time you guess the right color when the die is cast. If you were a fully rational being, you wouldn't guess at all, you would just say "yellow" every time. Since the rolls are not connected, the chances are equal for each and every roll. Chance says that for two thirds of the rolls, the outcome will be yellow. To maximize your winnings in the long run, you would have to go with yellow every time and win two thirds of the time. In reality, many people fall victim to the *predictable-world bias* and will try to *guess* each time what the color will be, thus losing more times than is necessary, not maximizing their results, but trying to be lucky.

In essence, predictable-world bias is to apply inductive reasoning when no such reasoning is warranted, since what you're trying to reason is in fact completely random. From an evolutionary point of view, it may well be that it gives an advantage to seek patterns and try and predict what's next, taking for granted that sometimes we become superstitious and see patterns where there are none.

What these biases – *availability, confirmation, predictable-world* – have in common, is that they might hinder problem solving in your organization. If the computer system goes down and you go look for the problem by sifting through the log files that are available to you, and you find entries that confirm your hunches, you might jump to the wrong conclusions. A smarter approach would be to consider what you don't know yet, leave the hunches out as much as you can, and use *deduction* instead to come to proper conclusions.

Deduction

Rather than draw a conclusion that *might* be true, based on bits and pieces of information (*induction*), *deduction* tries to arrive at a logical conclusion after careful observation and assessment of premises. If the premises are true, then the conclusion must also be true – if the reasoning is done correctly.

If all birds have feathers, and sparrows are birds, then sparrows must have feathers. If the premises – *all birds have feathers* and *sparrows are birds* – are true, then the conclusion that *sparrows must have feathers* is also true. This sort of puzzle is called a *syllogism*.

Deductive reasoning can also be applied to a *series problem*. Take, for instance, this:

Abdul is older than his sister Nora.

Abdul is younger than his brother Mo.

Mo is younger than his sister Hafsa.

Is Hafsa younger than Nora?

Just follow the steps and you'll find the answer is *no*. You've now used *deductive reasoning* to arrive at the answer.

It shouldn't surprise you that having great working-memory capacity helps when doing deductive reasoning.

Concrete Deductive Reasoning

You might have induced (pun intended) from the above paragraph that deductive reasoning is closely related to math. Just replace Abdul and Hafsa with X and Y, and there you go, a math problem that we can simply solve! It's not that simple however. In reality, we are usually much better able to reason with real-life examples than with abstract terms like X and Y. This has been shown in numerous studies by using real-life terms as abstract premises. As it turns out, no matter the intelligence, everybody solves problems faster if the words actually *mean* something.

There is a caveat however. We do have a bias towards *inductive* reasoning. So, even when a problem is served as a *deductive* reasoning problem, we tend to use our knowledge of the real world to induce certain information that might help us solve the problem. We do this quite automatically and it does not always help us solve the issue at hand.

For instance, take these sentences:

Men love sports.

Robin loves sports.

Therefore, Robin is a man.

The conclusion seems logical at first, but if you dig a little deeper – it states that men love sports, but it doesn't say that women don't like sports. It could very well be that Robin is a woman and that she does love sports. Our real-life understanding of the meaning of the words in combination with our own biases get in our way, by assuming men love sports more than women do. If you would mathematize this, it would be something like:

A loves X.

B loves X.

Therefore, B is an A.

This time it's quite clear the conclusion *might* be correct, but is not necessarily true.

Insight Problems

A special kind of reasoning is required to solve so-called *insight problems*. You might ponder for a long time on the solution to a problem, and after hours or even days of grinding your brains, all of sudden – there you have it! In German they call this an "*Aha!-Erlebnis*", and the ancient Greek mathematician Archimedes called out, "*Eureka!*" when he had an insight into the space occupied by water.

What separates insight problems from other problems, is the fact that you need to step out of your conventional thinking, your *mental set*, and "think outside the box". One of the more common limitations in thinking, is *functional fixedness*, when you can only see an object as having the use it normally has – whereas, to solve the problem, you might need to see the object used in a very different way. While functional fixedness *can* be a hindrance in solving difficult problems, usually it's actually a very useful bias, since it helps us in everyday life to make use of familiar (looking) items more quickly. With insight problems it's very helpful to leave the issue at hand for a while, and go and do something else in the meantime – this in between time is called the *incubation period*. When you come back to it, you're more likely to have your *Eureka!*-moment. What helps perhaps even more, is if you are very *creative*. Naturally creative people are more likely to solve insight problems faster. Getting people in a playful mood sparks their creativity, so making people laugh and play will definitely help them solve insight problems.

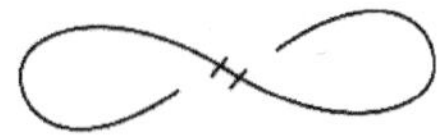

Chapter Three – The Self and Others

Now that we've established some essential inner workings of the self, it's time to have a closer look at how the self relates to others. For many, this is where the fun really starts! As a business coach, I mostly coach people in settings where they interact with one another – be it in a team, an entire work floor, or a whole organization. How do you fathom all the interactions taking place? Moreover, how do you *improve* the interactions and relations? First, we'll have to be able to recognize the different social environs.

The Basics of Social Psychology

The science that researches interpersonal relations is called *social psychology*. To understand human relations better, it's important to acknowledge that we were once not such a dominant species as we are today. Thousands of years ago, humans lived in groups – tribes – in order to simply *survive*. Being cast out of the tribe meant certain death for the individual. We grouped together to obtain food, for protection, and to make use of shared knowledge. In a group, each individual doesn't need to do, know, and remember everything – just as long as the group as a whole can take care of itself.

This last sentence might sound familiar to Agile-minded people since it could just as well be the description of an Agile team – the *team* needs to be able to take on anything coming at it. Within the team, the relationships between the individual team members can make or break the flow of the team. Social psychology examines relationships by looking at how we view each other and how we are influenced by one another.

Theory of Mind

Let's start intimate again, with the perception of others through the eyes of the *self*. Children up to the age of around three have a hard time relating to what others want or need, they see the world only through their eyes. When they grow older, they are able to understand what the world looks like through the eyes of the people around them. Being able to relate to the perceptions and thoughts of someone else is what psychologists have named *Theory of Mind*.

A great test to figure out how people think about the perception of others is the so-called *Sally and Anne test*. Image two girls, Sally and Anne, playing in the same room of a house. Sally has a basket with a ball in it and Anne has an empty box. Sally is playing with her ball and suddenly has to go to the toilet. She puts her ball in her basket and hurries to the toilet. Unbeknownst to Sally, while she is away, Anne picks the ball out of the basket and puts it in her box. When Sally returns, she wants to play with her ball again. Now, where do you think she will look first, in her basket, or in Anne's box? This will very likely seem like a simple question to you. Sally will look in her basket first, since that is where she left the ball before she went to the toilet. She has no reason to assume Anne took her ball, so the safest guess is exactly where she left it, in her basket. It turns out that children under the age of three will give exactly the *opposite* answer – they will say Sally will look inside the box. These children have seen with their very own eyes that Anne put the ball inside the box and they wholeheartedly take for granted that Sally will know this as much as they themselves know this to be true. The thought that the world might seem different from the perspective of Sally does not cross their minds.

It is interesting to know that people – also adults – who are on the *autistic spectrum* are more likely to say Sally will look inside the box first when she returns to the room. Being in the IT-business for several decades now, I know that people with autism are more likely to be found in IT than in other areas of work –

research has also shown this to be true. It will not come as a surprise to others who work in large organizations that quite a few IT people can be very *not-understanding* of people with less IT-knowledge than themselves. Rolling eyes and sighs of irritation are commonplace when lesser IT-savvy colleagues ask questions about the system that are so bloody obvious to the digital in-crowd – to whom it often seems very hard to understand why no one else gets what they see as such a simple truism. The next time you encounter such a situation, remember this paragraph – it might not be sheer arrogance, but rather the true inability to place oneself in another person's position.

Attributions

Theory of Mind enables us to relate to other people's thoughts and perceptions, but it – of course – does not help us *read* people's minds. Our *interpretations* of other people's personalities and intentions are based mostly on observing their *actions*. If someone smiles at us, we see the smile and interpret its meaning. Depending on the circumstances, the form of the smile, and the prior history we share with the smiler, we infer a meaning about the smile. What we ultimately conclude it to be – a friendly smile, a smirk, a feinted smile – will be added to our characterization of the smiler. Our conclusion about the observed (short-lived) behavior will help determine our conclusion about the (more permanent) characterization of their personality – like, "that's a friendly person", or, "that's a deceitful person". This process is called *making an attribution.*

Fundamental attribution error

Austrian social psychology pioneer Fritz Heider (1896-1988) noticed that people tend to give too much weight to *personality* in comparison with the *circumstances* someone finds themselves in at the moment. If we see someone laughing a lot, we easily conclude that the person is a cheerful person in general. We pay less attention to the fact that we observed this person on a Saturday night at a bar only. We don't know how that person is at home or at work, but we jump to characterization conclusions easily. This *person bias* has been proven to exist by so many experiments that psychologist Lee Ross (1942) named it the *fundamental attribution error* in 1977.

This common bias goes so far that experiments have shown that even if you divide a group of people *randomly* in two subgroups of *managers* and *clerks* and have them perform tasks accordingly, observers will rate the "managers" as higher in leadership, more intelligent, more assertive, et cetera. Even though the observers *knew* the assignment was random, the *fundamental attribution error* played its role and made them ignore that fact and have them attribute characteristics to people who had no effect on what behavior they could display under the circumstances.

We should be careful to recognize the fundamental attribution error when we observe people's behavior who have a certain role inside the organization. We might easily assume a tester is a very critical person who will always find something to nag about, just because they will display such behavior on a daily basis – exactly because it is their job to be critical and find every and any thing that is wrong with the (computer) system. That same tester might be a very lighthearted soccer coach in their spare time who runs a junior team of which they are not critical at all because it is all about the fun of play and sports to them.

Beautiful People

The erroneous attribution can go even further than judging a person solely on shortly observed behavior only – we also tend to derive characteristics from the *physical appearance* of someone. "Don't judge a book by its cover" is a saying that comes to mind when thinking of the *attractiveness bias*. Plenty of research has shown that we consider beautiful looking people to be friendlier, more intelligent, more competent, and even more moral. In one study, elementary school teachers were shown to rate attractive looking children as brighter and more successful than unattractive children, even though the kids had identical report cards. Other researchers looked at real court cases and found that judges regularly give unattractive people longer prison sentences than they give to attractive people, for comparable crimes.

The "funny" thing is that there actually *is* an iota of truth to the idea of beautiful people being smarter people. Research into attractiveness has shown that we consider people with more symmetrical faces to be more attractive. As it turns out, the less problems an unborn baby experiences while still in the womb, the more symmetrical its face will be. Thus, the idea goes, the more attractive a person looks, the more fit and healthy the person is, including their mental capacities. Some studies have shown that there actually is a very small – but still significant – relation between attractiveness and IQ, with attractive people having a higher IQ than unattractive people, although the attractiveness only accounts for about four percent of the variance.

Internet Connection

In these days of hyperconnectivity, the way we have and maintain relationships – also in our work environment – depends a lot more on the internet than it used to. As I'm writing this during the corona crisis, it is even more true than before. A study about differences between meeting people online and in real-life have shown a peculiar quirk. A group of participants in the study met new people face-to-face for the first time and then again face-to-face sometime after that. Another group met new people online for the first time (without sound, camera or photos – text only) and face-to-face for the second time. When asked how much they liked the new person they met, it turned out that after the first meeting, the people who met online liked the new person a whole lot more than the people who met each other in real-life. More interesting still, after the second meeting – for both groups the face-to-face meeting – the participants who first met online liked each other even more, a lot more, than the participants who only met in real-life – for them the liking even declined a bit. The researchers concluded that multiple factors were at play here. For one, the relative safety behind the keyboard – without seeing each other – gives way to more openness about the person's true self. Those participants were more open about their feelings and thoughts than the people who met in real-life, thus immediately creating an emotional bond. The people who didn't see each other at first also could not be biased by the looks of the new person, one way or the other. At the second meeting, the emotional bond could even result in seeing the new person as more attractive than if they had met as complete strangers.

I see a lot of people – both on social media as well as in organizations I work at – putting a lot of stress on having physical meetings as soon as possible. It would be wise to keep this research in mind and see the possible positive effects of first starting out online and then moving on to physical meetings.

On a personal side note, I actually met my wife through an online dating service, back in 2001. We corresponded through typed messages only for the first month or so, then spoke on the phone, but still we never even exchanged photographs. We saw each other physically for the first time after a few months of communication. Needless to say, I wholeheartedly concur the findings of the aforementioned research – still happy and going strong after being together almost twenty years already.

The Pygmalion Effect

We've gone from examining our *self* to making attributions to others. Now we'll add another step and see ourselves through the eyes of others. Research shows that our opinions and attitudes towards ourselves are a great deal affected by the opinions and attitudes of others. To a certain degree, the way others see us can actually become a new reality, whether there is truth to the way they see us to begin with or not. In other words, the expectations and beliefs of others about us, can become a *self-fulfilling prophecy*. In psychology, this phenomenon is called the *Pygmalion Effect*, after the mythical Roman sculptor who carved a statue of his ideal woman and brought her to life.

In a classic 1968 experiment by Robert Rosenthal and Lenore Jacobson, elementary school teachers were told that some of their students were shown by newly developed tests to go through an extraordinary intellectual growth-phase in the coming months. In reality, these little wonders of the classroom were picked randomly. It is also crucial to note here that the kids did *not* know they were being marked as special. After eight months, real IQ and other tests showed that these randomly picked kids had gained significantly more points in IQ and scored much better grades than their classmates. Researchers concluded that the mere beliefs and expectations of the teachers made the teachers create a better environment for these "special" students to thrive in. Also, through the different treatment by the teachers, the "special" kids actually *felt* special, which in turn increased their *self-image* and their *self-esteem*, ultimately resulting in better school results.

Many experiments have already shown that the *Pygmalion Effect* also applies to adults, and also in business settings. In short, if you treat your colleagues as if they were special, they will *feel* special, and in the end, they will *deliver* special. Surely something to keep in mind.

The Hawthorne Experiments

To elaborate on the Pygmalion Effect a little further, we'll have a look at the famous experiments held at the *Hawthorne Western Electric* plant in Illinois, from 1924 until 1932, which gave rise to what is now known as the *Hawthorne Effect*. Interestingly enough, and not known to many, *various* experiments were conducted at Hawthorne, led by different researchers and with different groups of workers.

It all began with the most famous Hawthorne study to determine if different intensities of light on the work floor would result in more or less productivity. After the light experiments, other variables were tried and tested, like cluttered or clean work stations, floors with or without obstacles, and complete relocation of work stations. In the early experiments, a group of six women who assembled telephone relays were put to the test. Their output (how many relays per hour they produced) was first secretly measured before they started working in a room that was built especially for the experiments. As it turned out, whenever *something* in the room was changed – be it the light-intensity or the cleanliness of the workstation – the women showed a short-lived *increase* of their output, even when the experimenters brought everything back to its original state, leaving the researchers in wonder. Participating researchers like Australian psychologist Elton Mayo (1880-1949) concluded that the workers came together as a real team and gave themselves wholeheartedly to the experiment, thus increasing their productivity.

In his 1958 book *Hawthorne Revisited*, researcher Henry A. Landsberger concluded that the increased attention by both the researchers and the management of Hawthorne, in combination with being part of a study, accounted for the temporary increases in productivity of the women. This conclusion has become widely known as the *Hawthorne Effect*.

Later critics, however, have doubted if there ever truly *was* a *Hawthorne Effect*. Some have called it a glorified anecdote with no data supporting the theory, while others try to explain the effect with what is called the *Demand Effect*, as described by psychologist and psychiatrist Martin Theodore Orne (1927-2000), in which subjects of a study interpret the purpose of the experiment and act accordingly.

Whatever the reality behind the Hawthorne experiments, the *Hawthorne Effect* is a famous description of the *Pygmalion Effect* on a group of people in a work environment setting – one of the first of its kind.

Self-esteem

We already slightly touched on the topic of self-esteem when discussing the *Pygmalion Effect* on the "special" school children, who increased their actual school results partly because of the improved environment and partly because of their increased self-esteem. Self-esteem is one's feeling of approval, acceptance, and liking of oneself. We *feel* our self-esteem is based on our own judgment of ourselves, but American psychologist Mark Leary (1954) proposed – in his *sociometer theory* – that the judgment is primarily based on our perceptions of other people's judgments of us. What you experience as your self-esteem, according to Leary, is your best guess of how much the people, whose opinion you care about, accept and respect you.

As evidence for this theory, Leary and others found – through research – that there is a strong correlation between self-esteem and the belief one is generally accepted by others. In further study of real-life experiences, people felt higher self-esteem after praise and social acceptance, and lower self-esteem after social rejection. The most convincing evidence came from a study into the question whether good or bad results on a test had any effect on self-esteem. As it turned out, the influence on self-esteem became a lot greater if the participant was made aware of other people learning about the test results. If self-esteem had been all about their own judgment, they wouldn't have cared what other people thought of their test results – since they did, it subscribes to the *sociometer theory*.

In modern work environments, people are encouraged to keep themselves up-to-date on the latest knowledge in their field of expertise, for instance by taking courses and earning certificates. The encouragement is often accompanied by an intrinsic incentive along the lines of, "you're doing this for yourself, for your own development". However true that may be concerning the obtained knowledge, the *sociometer theory* hints at highlighting the achievements to colleagues in order to boost the self-esteem of the student. So, put your colleagues on a pedestal every now and then and celebrate their accomplishments – because as we've seen before, increasing self-esteem will ultimately help in realizing better achievements.

Reference Groups

When we perceive other people's views of us, we handle different views differently. We actively value one view over another and even try to manipulate other people's views of us to try and influence our self-perception. Comparing ourselves to others is called *social comparison*, and the group of people we compare ourselves against is called the *reference group*. Our reference groups can differ a lot, depending on the social environment we find ourselves in. Thus, we feel different at work than at the sports club.

Research has shown that we tend to focus on traits that set us apart from the rest of the group. When thinking about yourself at work, we might focus on being the only woman on the team, or being the youngest team member, while at the sports club, we might focus on being the slowest, or the strongest. If you play sports in a women-only team, it doesn't cross your mind that you're a woman, because the entire reference group is also female. Likewise, at work it won't cross your mind that you can type pretty fast, since all your colleagues can do that as well.

It should come as no surprise that how we relate to a reference group has a big influence on our self-esteem. If you measure yourself against team members who are better at everything you are good at, your best guess will be no respect and perhaps little acceptance from the others. On the other hand, if your abilities generally align with the team, and you stand out in a thing or two, then your best guess will be both acceptance and respect. Since our achievements are influenced by our self-esteem, it's possible someone performs terribly in one team and thrives in another. It's important to notice that being better at everything than everyone else on your team will also impede the acceptance and liking part that partly forms the basis of your self-esteem, even though the respect part might still play a big role.

From my point of view, as a coach who is often involved in team coaching, what I've described here – about reference groups and self-esteem – is not taken into account enough in organizations. When teams are formed, the usual first aspect to consider is the technical expertise, after which the coach, team lead, or Scrum Master are expected to work on the *team building* to make the team "work". Following the popular 2002 book *The Five Dysfunctions of a Team* by American business consultant Patrick Lencioni (1965) about how to create *high-performance teams* in an organization, much stress is put on building *trust,* seeking constructive – yet critical – dialogue, forming commitment, promoting responsibility, and focusing on team results. None of these steps is truly possible if the self-esteem of the team members is below par. For instance, Lencioni describes building trust by sharing personal stories. You will, however, not trust your team members with your inner feelings and most personal stories if you feel no acceptance, no respect, and no liking – in other words, if your self-esteem around this reference group is at an all-time low. In my opinion it would be wise to look at forming teams from a perspective of *reference groups* and *self-esteem,* especially since an increase in self-esteem has a direct effect on personal and – by extension – team performance.

Self-serving Attributional Bias

However potent the influence of reference groups is, we are stubborn creatures as well. Most of us feel pretty good about ourselves and often not entirely based on reality. Many studies throughout the years have shown that people tend to think of themselves as better than average. For instance, and you might recognize this, most people think of themselves as better car drivers than others. This unrealistic view of our own abilities permeates throughout almost every aspect of our lives. From a psychological health point of view, this *positive illusory bias* is not such a bad thing – it feels good to think well of yourself.

As we saw in relation to the reference groups, we value different information differently. This is especially true if we value information about ourselves compared to information about others. We already noticed that the *fundamental attribution error* makes us see actions of others a result of their personality rather than the circumstances. We don't do this when it comes to our own actions. When judging our own behavior, we tend to attribute successes to our personality, but our failures to the circumstances. This bias is aptly named the *self-serving attributional bias*. You can often see this bias at work in sports, where, whenever a team wins, they worked hard and are just *that* good, but when they lose, the referee was against them and the other team engaged in foul play. We can see this at work as well, when, if a team did well, they celebrate working hard and being smart, but if they underperformed, the computer system failed, the other teams were holding them up, management didn't support them – anyway, you probably recognize some of these excuses.

This self-serving bias also extends into our memories. Research has shown that we tend to remember our successes a lot better than our failures, while this does not count for the successes and failures of others.

Overall, it's good to think positively about yourself, but when you think *too* positively about yourself and it's *not* based on matching achievements, the self-serving bias becomes a problem. As we've seen with the topic of *toxic positivity*, the one-sided focus on the positive makes people shy away from the realities of failure and loss, while the underlying feelings still linger in the background. At one point or another, the unattended emotions will come to the surface, and sometimes in detrimental ways. Adjustment problems, including depression, might be the result. Especially with young people, the focus – from their environment – on establishing high self-esteem through positive thinking, might result in major blowback when they don't have matching achievements to go with their inflated self-esteem. When failure eventually hits, depression lurks around the corner.

Attitudes

We've been talking about attributions, perceptions, views, et cetera. If a way of seeing others or ourselves is accompanied by an *evaluative* aspect, psychologists speak of an *attitude*. We constantly judge persons, actions, ideas, but also things or events, as being good or bad, likable or unlikable, attractive or repulsive, moral or immoral. The attitudes we care for the most are our *values*. Early social psychologists like Gordon Allport (1897-1967) – whom we encountered when discussing *traits* in the previous chapter – studied attitudes to see if they would predict how someone would behave under certain circumstances. One major finding is the difference between *explicit* and *implicit* attitudes.

We actively maintain *explicit attitudes* and express them verbally and consciously – we are aware of these attitudes and cultivate them. For instance, in a work environment, you might maintain the attitude that decision making should take place at the lowest possible levels in the organization and that there should be as few levels as possible anyway – very much in line with popular Agile-minded theories around organizational structuring, like the idea of a "Teal organization" as presented by Belgian organizational consultant Frederic Laloux (1969) in his 2014 book *Reinventing Organizations*. Whenever discussions arise around decision making, you promote your attitude that the decision making should take place on the work floor rather than in the ivory management tower.

We also maintain *implicit attitudes*. These attitudes manifest themselves as automatic mental associations that influence our behavior unconsciously. A great test that psychologists have devised is to measure the time that is needed to associate two words. If the time is short, the two words are easily mentally connected and the association is called strong. If you're quicker to associate the word "management" with positive words like "intelligent", "hard-working", or "decisive", than to associate the word "management" with negative words like "short-sighted", "dictatorial", or "self-serving", then your *implicit attitude* towards management is *positive*. If you responded quicker to the negative words, that means your *implicit attitude* towards management is *negative*. Mostly, our explicit and implicit attitudes coincide, in which cases our behavior is predictable to ourselves and to others. But still quite often, our explicit and implicit attitudes differ, and that's when things get interesting.

Research shows that the *less* we think about our behavior, the more our *implicit* attitudes play a defining role in it. So, if your explicit attitude towards decision making tends towards Laloux' ideas about organizational structure, but your implicit attitude tells you that management is better equipped to make decisions, on a hectic day, you might simply go with the traditional flow in the organization and let management decide upon an important issue, whereas, on a quieter day – with plenty of room to think – you object and start asking hard questions about where the decision making should take place, with management, or rather, on the work floor. In other words, by thinking and contemplating, our explicit attitudes can *override* our implicit attitudes.

Cognitive Dissonance

When we become aware of inconsistencies between our *explicit attitudes* and other information – be it our own behavior or facts that are new to us – we perceive an uncomfortable feeling. In 1957, American social psychologist Leon Festinger (1919-1989) named this feeling *cognitive dissonance* – which to this day remains one of the most significant aspects of social psychology.

Since we want to get rid of the discomfortable feeling, *cognitive dissonance* makes us rethink our explicit attitudes. Did we make a mistake in our thinking and should we adjust our explicit attitudes, or are the new facts not actual facts? Or perhaps it's a bit of both? Whatever the outcome, by responding to the inconsistencies, we might well be addressing an issue that could have become a real problem if left unattended. Despite the somewhat negative-sounding word *dissonance*, *cognitive dissonance* is usually a good thing that helps us adapt to – and survive – the changing world around us.

Sometimes, *cognitive dissonance* leads to less desirable thinking and behavior. For instance, when we receive new information that doesn't rhyme with our explicit attitude, but we persist in maintaining that attitude against all better judgment. If your explicit attitude towards the COVID-19 coronavirus had been all along that it is a benign virus, not worse than ordinary flu, you might try to avoid any news that is related to the rising death toll, and instead only focus on news that downplays the death toll or simply avoid the news at all in order to lessen the feeling of *cognitive dissonance*.

Perhaps less destructive, but nonetheless self-deceiving, is the tendency to affirm our explicit attitudes once we've passed a point of no return. For instance, imagine you're wondering about leaving the company you work for, but are still pretty much in doubt because your attitude towards a new employer is not absolutely positive and your attitude about your current employer is not that negative. In spite of your doubts, you take a leap of faith, quit your current job and start working for the new employer. What research has shown, is that – after your job change – you are likely to downplay your doubts and affirm the positive attitude towards the new employer in order to dissipate the discomfortable feeling you have – even in the absence of new information.

If we take the example of the decision making in the organization, you might have gone along with a management decision one day and lie awake that night wondering why you didn't object during the day – your explicit attitude should have told you to object, but you didn't. If you can't think of a good reason why you didn't object, the *insufficient-justification effect* might persuade you to alter your explicit attitude – you might even "switch sides" and maintain that important decisions, like those on the table that day, *should* be made by management, just to ease the uncomfortable feeling of dissonance.

In-groups and Out-groups

We've talked about reference groups as a group of people we compare ourselves against. We often find ourselves in groups, since we humans are social beings, as they say. We live in families, we attend school, we join a sports team or club, we work with others, and we join leisure time groups, like a music band. We could also be part of groups that usually don't come together physically as an entire group, like when you're a member of a political party, or as part of an unofficial group of fans of a certain movie star. We are part of many different groups and sometimes we are part of smaller groups inside a larger group. You might, for example, be part of the coaches group in the organization you work at. When we identify with a certain group, psychologists call that our *social identity* – as opposed to our *personal identity*, which relates to us as a separate individual. The group we identify with is called the *in-group*, while the group we don't belong to is considered the *out-group*. Because we switch from group to different group all the time, beware that someone else might be in the *in-group* one moment, and in the *out-group* the next.

When we see ourselves – or others – as part of a group, we tend to overlook the individual differences and see the group members as similar to each other. That is the case even more so when we observe *out-groups*.

Stereotypes & Prejudice

In our minds, we create a *schema* of a group – a mixed set of knowledge and beliefs about that group. These schemas, called *stereotypes*, are related to *prejudice* and have a negative connotation, which is not necessarily correct. Stereotypes are very useful in our everyday life.

As a matter of fact, we would probably not survive without prejudice or stereotypes. From likeness to other members of the same group we infer meaning that is often correct. For instance, if we see an apple, we are not likely to have ever seen this particular apple, and maybe not even this species of apple, but we recognize it as part of the group of fruit which are apples. From this likeness we infer that we can eat the apple and that it will be sweet and tasty. It might be a poisonous apple, but that is not very likely. We see a piece of furniture that resembles a chair and we infer from its likeness to other furniture in the group of chairs that we can sit on it. The chair might collapse, but in all likeliness, we can sit on it. If we'd have to investigate and test every chair before sitting down, meetings at work would take even more time than they already do. Instead, our prejudice about chairs is probably right. The stereotype of a chair as a piece of furniture you can sit on will be correct most of the times throughout your life.

The trouble arises when the stereotype is wrong and based not on facts, but on exaggerated or fabricated characterizations of a group – then we make inferences that will not hold true for the individual of that group. This is of course where the negative connotation comes from – when we prejudge a person based on false characterizations formed by social or cultural misconceptions or deliberate mischaracterizations.

Just like with explicit and implicit *attitudes*, there are explicit and implicit *stereotypes*. Again, the *implicit stereotype* is hidden from your conscious but does play a role in forming your behavior. Psychologists generally split the explicit stereotype in two parts – one of them the *public explicit stereotype* and the other the *private explicit stereotype*. The public stereotype is the public view that you openly share with others, while the private stereotype is the view of a group that you consciously have, but don't like to share with the world. Implicit stereotypes can be found through a test that is similar to the test that is used to find implicit attitudes. When certain words are quickly associated with a group, the association is strong. When "good" words are quickly associated with the group, then the stereotype is a *positive stereotype*, and vice versa, when "bad" words are more quickly associated with the group, the stereotype is a *negative stereotype*.

One common stereotype found in Western countries is the stereotype of black people being bad in some way. Extensive research has shown that *most* people in Western countries are at the very least *implicitly* biased against black people. The troubling outcome of these studies shows that even black people have implicit biases against black people. Even more worrisome is that these implicit biases already occur at a very young age – children as young as six years old implicitly associate black people with "bad" and white people with "good". Next to the coronavirus, the year

2020 will probably be remembered for the totally unnecessary and brutal murder of George Floyd, African American, by the hands – or rather the knee – of a white police officer. Following the gruesome asphyxiation of Floyd, a worldwide call for justice swelled, using the rallying cry "black lives matter". The research on stereotypes shows that even though most people maintain a *public explicit stereotype* about black people that says black people are equal in every respect to white people, and even though many people will also maintain a *private explicit stereotype* that says the same, our *implicit stereotype* says otherwise. And as we've seen with attitudes, *thinking* and *contemplating* gives power to explicit stereotypes to *override* implicit stereotypes. This is exactly what "black lives matter" is all about, making people consciously aware of the implicit stereotype. People that state we should all simply say that "all lives matter", incorrectly negate the effect on our behavior of the *implicit stereotype*.

In our work environments we encounter plenty of negative stereotypes, besides the omnipresent bias against black people. Women, gay people, transgender people, people with disabilities, but also (relatively) old people – there are many groups of people inside our organizations that suffer in one way or another from negative stereotypes on a daily basis. Studies have shown that it can take a long time to overcome negative stereotypes, especially the implicit kind. What research suggests helps best, is not just to learn more about the outgroups (the groups you don't belong to), but also to mingle with them – get to know persons from those groups, as *individuals*. When you make friends with people that belong to a group you have a negative (implicit) bias against, that bias will slowly but surely decline.

Social Pressure

No matter how individualistic someone may seem, no one is uninfluenced by others. How we behave depends not only on who we are, but also upon which social environment we find ourselves in. When others are mentally or physically close to us, they exert certain demands, expectations, judgments, and examples on us – whether real or imagined by us. That is what we call *social pressure*.

Even though it doesn't sound like it, *social pressure* can be a good thing – just like stereotypes or prejudice – since it helps create predictable and orderly social interactions. *Social pressure* turns sour when it makes us behave stupidly or even morally wrong.

Social facilitation and social interference

A very minimal form of *social pressure* is having people watch you while you perform tasks. Sometimes people observing us improves our performance and then it's called *social facilitation*. When people watching us deteriorates our performance, it's called *social interference.*

Polish-American social psychologist Robert Zajonc (1923-2008) noticed through his many experiments that *social facilitation* usually occurs with relatively simple or well-learned tasks, while *social interference* mostly occurs with complex or relatively new tasks. What is simple to one, might be complex to the other, so you can't simply say that one task or another will invoke either social facilitation or social interference. One experiment showed that expert pool players benefited from a critical audience and improved their performance while being observed closely, while novice pool players saw their performance drop when observed by a stern-looking audience.

Another interesting experiment showed that you don't even have to have the audience present when you perform the tasks in order to feel the social pressure. Students that were given negative feedback just before asked to explain something new, felt a lot less confident and fared a lot worse than their classmates who were given positive feedback right before being asked to do the same. Apparently, the social pressure works both ways, even from a distance and through time – definitely something to keep in mind at work, also in times of working remotely.

Choking under pressure

We've probably all experienced the phenomenon of *choking*. When doing an exam that you just can't allow yourself to fail, or in a high-stakes sports event during the closing minutes. You feel stressed out and just can't seem to think straight anymore. The *social interference* that was just mentioned is a special case of *choking under pressure*. Research into *choking under pressure* has revealed that our *working memory* plays a big role in it. We've seen in the previous chapter – about the self – that our working memory is pretty limited – you're able to hold about seven, plus or minus two, chunks of data in your working memory. When you don't actively work with the chunks, they fleet from memory within a couple of seconds.

When the (social) pressure is on and you work on something very difficult or relatively new to you, your working memory is distracted by thoughts of failure, of being watched and judged, about the difficulty of the problem, et cetera. Since your working memory is already limited, the worries and anxiety taking up space limit it even further, which in turn worsens your performance.

At work we run the risk of *choking under pressure* when things don't go as planned and managers start breathing down the necks of people who actually need to do the job. I've seen it happen so many times. The application should go live for thousands of users worldwide in a couple of days and we still need to fix this annoying bug that turned up in a crucial part of the application. The team has already figured out in which area of the code the bug resides, and it so happens that no one but Joe knows that particular area. All eyes on Joe. And Joe feels the eyes of his colleagues burning in his back. Word about the bug has reached the higher levels of management and even though those managers are rarely interested in what the developers do and deliver, now – of all times – they are interested. Some manager just happens to be in the building and pass by – what a coincidence – and starts asking questions here and there. Not before long, Joe not only feels his peers' but also the manager's eyes burning a hole in his back. Joe is sweating and starts to go numb. He's not typing anymore, he's just scrolling with his mouse, scrolling up and down through endless lines of code. The bug should be here somewhere. Deadline after deadline passes and Joe forfeits – he calls it quits and goes home, leaving everyone in disarray. The next day, when the final deadline has passed and management has decided to postpone the entire thing, Joe finds the bug within an hour.

The lesson here is to leave the *working memory* available to be able to solve problems. One obvious part of the solution is to keep the social pressure off by keeping management at bay. In an Agile environment, that's part of the job of a Scrum Master or an Agile Coach. You can keep the peer pressure off by approaching the problem solving as a team effort. Even though the other team members might not know the particular technical aspects surrounding the issue, they are able to support by asking stupid questions which will make Joe's thoughts explore new avenues, or simply to sit next to Joe and do nothing but show their support and letting Joe know they're in this together.

Stereotype threat

A special type of *choking under pressure* is called *stereotype threat*. Research by American social psychologist Claude Steele (1946) has shown that people who know they are subject to negative stereotyping do worse on tests related to that stereotype, especially if they were just made aware of the stereotype. Women, for instance, are generally stereotyped as being worse at math than men. If women are made aware of their gender just before taking a math test, by having to fill in their gender at the top of the test sheet, they perform worse on the test than women who were not made aware of their gender, and worse than women who were told that gender has no effect on math test performance.

Besides being a specific type of *choking under pressure*, the *stereotype threat* is also a form of a *self-fulfilling prophecy* – thinking you're going to perform badly causes you to actually perform badly. Therefore, in our modern – heavily IT-dependent organizations – we should all be aware of the *stereotype threat* effect of general stereotypes regarding women and computers, for instance, or stereotypes about older people and computers. As the research shows, the *stereotype threat* can be easily mitigated by simply addressing the effect and making people aware of it. Also, addressing people's strengths boosts their self-esteem which in turn lessens the effect of the *stereotype threat*.

Impression Management

Besides being influenced by others in the form of *social pressure*, we also tend to *actively work* on how others perceive and judge us. As mentioned in the segment about reference groups, our self-esteem – and therewith our performance – is derived from the acceptance and respect we feel from the social environment we find ourselves in at that moment. While we *feel* differently in different groups, we also *act* differently in different groups. Behaving differently to influence other people's perceptions is called *impression management*.

Being the social beings that we are, we need others to achieve our long-term goals in life and part of convincing others to collaborate with us is making a *good impression* – whatever "good" is for the particular reference group, but usually things like being trustworthy, friendly, competent, et cetera. We sometimes act in accordance with the good impression consciously, but more often than not, we are natural born actors who unconsciously know how to play the part. Studies have shown that we are busier with *impression management* when meeting new people than when we are around friends and familiar faces. Good to take this into account when someone new joins the team, or when a whole new team is formed – the behavior of the team members might be the result of *conscious impression management.*

Influence by Example

Next to the social pressure, we are also heavily influenced by *examples* that others set. There are basically two kinds of *influence by example.* You can observe someone behave in a way that tells you they probably know more than you do about something and you subsequently follow their lead because you trust that they behave that way on purpose and with good intent. Let's say you're new at a job and everyone avoids the coffee machine on the first floor and goes out of their way to the second floor to get a cup of coffee first thing in the morning. You automatically follow their example and get your hot cup of coffee on the second floor when you arrive the next day – without really knowing why. You just assume that if people go through the extra trouble of going to the second floor to get a cup of coffee, it must be a whole lot better than the coffee on the first floor. This sort of influence is called *informational influence*.

When you follow other people's examples because you feel a need to fit in the group, it's called *normative influence*. Let's say everyone in the office wears a suit and you're not used to that, but you change your habit and start wearing a suit as well, you follow the ideas and habits of the group to find approval and fit right in.

Conformity

If you are heavily influenced by the group you take part in, to the extent that you are willing to submit to the leading opinion in the group, we talk of *conformity*. In the 1950s, pioneering Polish-American social psychologist Solomon Asch (1907-1996) conducted now famous experiments on conformity which played out differently from what he thought they would. Asch hypothesized that people would *not* conform to the opinion of a group if the objective evidence showed that the opinion was a clear-cut falsehood. It was surprising to Asch that the opposite turned out to be true. I must say, try looking up some videos of these experiments – which have been replicated by others numerous times – and be amazed by what happens. The general idea of the experiments is the following. A group of people is shown a first card with a line drawn on it of a certain length. Then another card is shown, with three lines on it, all of different length. Only one of the three lines equals the line on the first card in length. The group members are asked one by one which of three lines matches the first card's line. As you can see in the image below, the answer is pretty obvious.

Asch's conformity experiment

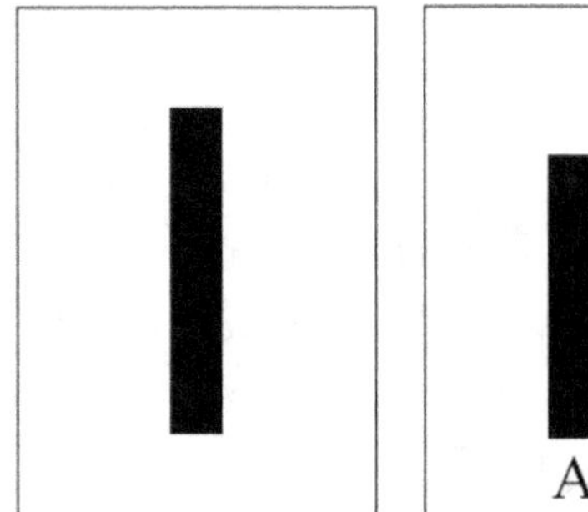
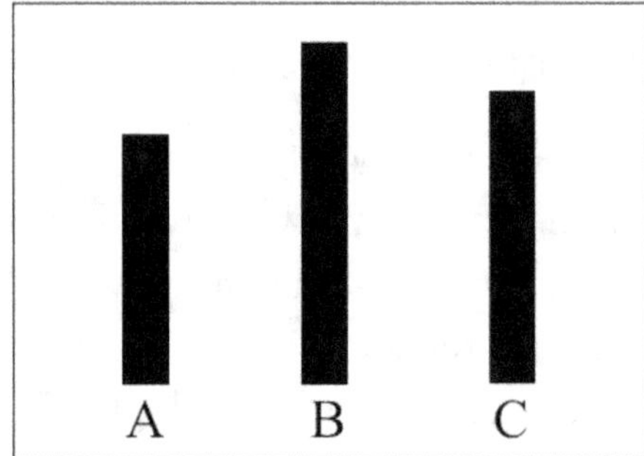

The trick of the experiment is that there is only *one* test subject in the group, who is unaware of being that only one. The subject is usually seated at the far right side of the group and the researcher asks the person on the far left side first which of the three lines matches the line on the first card. Let's say the obvious correct answer is – as in the above image – answer C. All persons of the group are what they call "confederates", usually students cooperating with the researcher, but at least people who are acting on behalf of the study taking place. The real test subject is never aware of the confederates being in on the conspiracy. The confederate on the far left answers, "A". The confederate sitting next to him also says "A", and so on. Until we meet the real test subject at the right side of the group. What will the participant answer, the obvious correct answer "C", or will they answer in harmony with the group, and say "A"? It turns out that most people will start out with a bit of a chuckle and give the correct answer. At least for the first few rounds. Multiple cards with three lines are held up by the researcher and each time all confederates answer wrongly. In the videos, you can see the test subject deeply wondering why the others give the so blatantly wrong answers. But after a few rounds of being shown different cards, many grow tired of opposing the groups' opinion. There are people who keep resisting and stick with their own (correct) views, but most participants collapse – and faster than you'd think. It's funny and tragic at the same time to see that some don't even look at the cards anymore, they simply repeat what the people before them say.

If you're used to Agile ways of working in your organization, you'll probably know the practice of *Poker Planning*. A team will estimate the effort it will take to complete a piece of work using cards the size of playing cards, with numbers on them; 0, ½, 1, 2, 3, 5, 8, 13, 20, 40, and 100. This range sort of resembles the *Fibonacci sequence* – for those familiar with math – in which each number is the sum of the two previous numbers (0, 1, 1, 2, 3, 5, 8, 13, 21, 34, 55, etc.). Each team member will pick a card with a number which they think matches the relative amount of work needed to complete a certain set of tasks. The team will usually start out with some sort of example piece of work, which they will give a number, for instance, 3. Every next set of work that is being discussed, is compared against the first, against the 3. So, if a piece of work seems to be twice as much work as the first one, the team members might pick a 5 or an 8, after which a discussion usually follows about why some people chose a 5 and others an 8, and some might have picked a completely different number, like 3 or 13, which is food for conversation. The main aspect of this ritual of *Poker Planning*, is that all team members show the card they picked to the other team members *at the very same time*. This part of the ritual is directly related to the research of Asch. With it, the team prevents its members from conforming mindlessly to the opinion of others – and thus, to the opinion of the quickest, loudest, or most experienced person in the group.

Theory X & Y

In 1960, American management professor Douglas McGregor (1906-1964) – who was a student of the famous American psychologist Maslow – expounded in his book *The Human Side of Enterprise* that there are basically two sorts of theories about management and motivation, which he named Theory X and Theory Y.

Theory X assumes the average employee is quite lazy, avoids responsibility, has little ambition, and is in it mainly for the money – a steady income. Managers who adhere to this theory, are more likely to trust mainly in supervision and use rewards and penalties to try and motivate their employees. Theory Y, on the other hand, assumes the average employee works pretty hard, is intrinsically motivated, enjoys their job, and wants to improve themselves – no matter the monetary rewards. Managers who believe in Theory Y, typically take a more personal approach to their employees and trust them to do a good job without much supervision. I'm sure you can recognize the more traditional management in Theory X, and more modern approaches – like Agile and Lean – in Theory Y.

The opposing theories have been – and still are – very influential in many organizations, probably because they are so opposing and so recognizable at the same time. I doubt if you can find managers who adhere to Theory X *only*, or ones that adhere to Theory Y *only*, but I'm sure you will recognize tendencies towards one of the opposing theories in both others and yourself.

Obedience

One year after McGregor published his Theory X & Y, American psychologist Stanley Milgram began his now famous experiments on *obedience to authority.* Milgram was Jewish and very intrigued by the trail of Nazi Adolf Eichmann, one of the main orchestrators of the Holocaust who had been captured by the Israeli secret service – the Mossad – in Argentina in 1960. Eichmann was subsequently put on trial in Jerusalem and defended his actions that resulted in the murder of millions of people by saying he was "simply following orders". Milgram was intrigued by this defence and wanted to see if average, normal people would follow orders to kill a fellow – innocent – human being when ordered to do so by an authority figure.

The experiment Milgram concocted involved one subject. This participant, however, would assume to be part of an experiment along with another subject. The goal of the fake experiment was to learn about the influence of punishment on learning. One subject would be the student, and the other the teacher. Picking who would be the student and who would be the teacher would seem random to the participant, but was in fact rigged – the subject would *always* become the teacher.

The "student" would have to memorize 300 pairs of words. After that, in the actual experiment setting, the teacher would say one half of the pair out loud to the student, and the student would have to reply the other half. If the student was not able to do so, the teacher would have to apply a punishment to incentivise the student. The punishment was an electrical shock. The first shock would be a very small and benign shock. With every mistake, however, the voltage of the shock – and therefore the severity of the shock – would increase. Of course, the shocks weren't real, but the "teacher" didn't know that. In the experiment setting, the student would be placed in an adjacent room, out of sight of the teacher. As far as the teacher knew, the student was strapped to a chair, with electrical wire attached to his arm, ready to receive the punishing shocks if he made mistakes. The teacher had a microphone in front of him, as well as a giant board with dozens of switches with the number of Volts indicating how severe the administered shock would be if the switch was pulled. There were also additional texts on the board, like, "DANGER: SEVERE SHOCK".

Interestingly enough, Milgram conducted a poll *before* starting his experiments at Yale University. He asked psychology seniors and his colleagues from Yale, as well as psychiatrists from a medical school, how far they thought the participants would go with the experiment until they would refuse to pull the switches. All of them predicted only a very small portion of the participants would continue to the end of the experiment – applying the maximum voltage. On average, they predicted only a few percent. Milgram himself assumed Americans would refuse much sooner than would Germans. He planned on doing the same experiments with German participants, basically to be able to show that Germans would be more inclined to follow orders, but wanted to do the control tests with Americans first. Milgram never made it to German participants.

The results of the experiments with the average American participants were so shocking that the filmed footage of the experiments is mesmerizing to see even to this day. You can easily find the documentary that Milgram released later – named *Obedience* – on the internet, which shows the blood-curling footage of "students" screaming of pain and "teachers" continuing to pull the switches – until there is no sound coming out of the room next door. Of the first group of participants, a whopping 65 percent went all the way and administered the more than deadly 450-Volt shock. *All* of them – the full 100 percent – administered shocks of the already potentially lethal 300 Volts.

What is important here is the role of the "experimenter" – the *authority* figure. The subjects were never alone in the room, there was always a man in the room with a white lab coat on – the supposed researcher testing his hypothesis about learning through punishments. Whenever the teachers hesitated, verbally objected, or refused to continue, the lab coat guy insisted that the teacher continued the experiment. At first he would say sentences like, "please continue", or, "please go on", but after a few more rounds, when that incentive would not suffice anymore with the resisting subject, he would say things like, "the experiment requires you continue", "it is absolutely essential that you continue", and, "you have no other choice, you must go on". Apparently, these words were enough to entice most subjects into submission and to continue to torture their victim. Remember this all seemed very real to them – as far as they knew, the guy in the other room was truly in severe pain and distress, right up the point of *dying* during the experiment.

Much to the shock (no pun intended) of Milgram, he realized that "relatively few people have the resources needed to resist authority". Milgram's experiment on *obedience to authority* has been repeated often and worldwide, the results being almost the same everywhere. If you're thinking, well, that was in 1961, surely nowadays people are less inclined to be obedient to authority figures, then guess again. Experiments like these are still being carried out worldwide, and still the results show the same everywhere, every time. The only real difference between Milgram's originals and today's experiments is that the effects on the participants are nowadays taken into account. Since the subjects think they are administering real shocks, after the experiment, they have to live with the idea that they are capable of torturing and perhaps even killing a real innocent human being. The very burden of that realization is today considered to be torture in itself. Hence, most experiments are stopped at a certain voltage by the experimenters, since earlier studies have already shown that if "teachers" go beyond a certain voltage, they are likely to go to the end.

What can we – working in modern organizations – learn from Milgram's groundbreaking experiment? Too often, managers and executives inside organizations don't realize the power of their authority. As former CEO J.P. Garnier of pharmaceutical company GlaxoSmithKline put it, "I've learned that my *suggestions* become *orders*". I've heard more than one executive complain – behind closed doors – that nobody in the organization stopped them from taking a stupid decision. "Why didn't anybody tell me?" Well, the *authority* your role carries, prevents people from speaking up, even if they know you're blatantly wrong. As a leader – formal or informal – you need to be aware of the weight of your words. Your authority can come in handy at times, but the flipside can be tricky at best, and detrimental at worst.

Autonomy, Mastery, and Purpose

In the last decades we've seen a slow but sure transition from a world of *authoritative command-and-control* to a new equilibrium of *cooperative self-organization* inside larger organizations. American author Daniel Pink (1964) argues – in his 2009 book *Drive: The Surprising Truth About What Motivates Us* – that if work goes beyond the most rudimentary cognitive levels, monetary rewards won't cut it to incite more motivation for the person doing the work. Instead, Pink propounds, research from the Massachusetts Institute of Technology (MIT), the University of Chicago, and Carnegie Mellon – and sponsored by the US Federal Reserve Bank – shows that what actually motivates people are *autonomy, mastery,* and *purpose.*

If the worries over basic needs are mitigated by a decent income, people are motivated to increase their performance when they feel they have a say in what work is done, and how and when it is done. The feeling of being able to have a degree of autonomy over your work motivates you to engage more and ultimately, perform better. Another aspect is mastery. If you're allowed and encouraged to increase your skills on the work floor, that helps in motivating you to do better overall. Thirdly, having a true meaningful and important long-term goal is an important aspect of creating motivation for employees. If you feel you're coming to work every day to make the world a better place, that motivates a whole lot more than simply working to increase the profits for the shareholders.

While it's quite easy to recognize the importance of *autonomy, mastery,* and *purpose* – also perhaps for your own motivation at work – it still is hard in today's organizations to get around the more traditional forms of rewards (and maybe even punishments) used to "motivate" people – like end-of-the-year bonuses, or the withdrawal thereof. Unfortunately, change – even backed up by decent research – seems inherently slow inside larger organizations.

Social Norms

When we take part in any social setting, we notice that people do certain things in specific ways. We can tell what is considered to be "normal" by the group and what is not. These what we call *social norms* are of great influence on our own behavior. Because we deal with *social norms* inside organizations as well – as part of the *company culture* – I want to highlight one specific aspect of social norms, and that is the power – or the lack thereof – of *public messages.* All too often, management sends out company-wide messages to stimulate a certain type of behavior, or vice versa, to discourage certain behavior. If you don't do this right, the results might be exactly the opposite of what you are aiming for.

American professor of psychology and marketing – and persuasion expert – Robert Cialdini (1945), worked with the Petrified Forest National Park in Arizona to see how they could prevent people from taking petrified wood out of the forest – in other words, to prevent stealing – by using different signs near the entrance of the forest. One message they tried out, read, "Many past visitors have removed petrified wood from the park, changing the natural state of the Petrified Forest", while another version read, "Please do not remove the petrified wood from the Park, in order to preserve the natural state of the Petrified Forest". As a control setting, they also tested what happened when they didn't place a sign at all. As it turned out, without a sign, about 3% of the visitors illegally took petrified wood with them. When the first sign was tried out – with the "many past visitors have removed" – a shocking almost 8% of the Park's visitors stole petrified wood from the Forest. The other sign – the "please do not remove" – resulted in a lot less stealing – less than 2% took some petrified wood in that case. As Cialdini pointed out, the "*many past visitors* have removed petrified wood" resulted in setting a *social norm* of "stealing is quite common and considered normal over here", which resulted in more *actual* theft. On the other hand, the "please do not remove the petrified wood, in order to preserve the natural state"-sign resulted in a much better outcome than no sign at all. Apparently, by conveying the rarity of theft, this message set a totally different social norm, namely that stealing is not normal.

If you're part of the leadership in the organization, you better be careful in setting the tone of social norms by sending public messages into the company – a difference between less than 2% and almost 8% is significant by any standard, and could be crucial in a company-wide transformation process. If you want people to follow the new guidelines, you might want to avoid a message that says, "we see that not enough people are following the new guidelines and that really needs to improve", and go for the alternative, "we see that almost everyone is following the new guidelines already, so we're confident that pretty soon everyone will be following the guidelines" – thus highlighting what is "the new normal" by stressing both the numbers ("almost everyone") and that the "new guidelines" are actually "*the* guidelines".

The Bystander Effect

What if there is no authority around? In modern organizations there is a growing tendency to strive for more *autonomy* and *self-organization*, for both teams and for individuals inside teams. Teams should be able to determine what work they can handle and how they accomplish that. The ideas behind the growing autonomy is both the aforementioned advantages of the motivation for employees as well as the high level of expertise that lives inside the teams – much of today's work has become so technically complicated that managers no longer have the knowledge nor the skills to determine what other people can or cannot do, how they do it, and how much effort that will take. Also, in modern organizations, there is no longer a strict hierarchy present *inside* teams. Take, for instance, a modern Agile framework like *Scrum*, in which there are only three roles in a team – *Product Owner*, *Scrum Master*, and *Development Team Member*. There is no "Project Manager", "Team Lead", "Senior Developer", "Team Architect", "Test Lead", et cetera. All team members are considered to be equal and are equally held responsible for the end result which is achieved by the team.

In both life outside work and at work, we seldom find ourselves in situations where *no one* is in charge, but it does happen. Textbook examples are situations where someone on the street is in distress and there is no police or other authority around (yet). A classic example, which you will find in any psychology textbook, is the New Yorker murder case of Kitty Genovese. The 28-year-old was stabbed to death in the early morning of March 13, 1964, a few feet from her apartment building. She came home late from her work at a bar and parked near the entrance of her apartment building in an alley. She was followed home and on the doorsteps of her apartment building, she was stabbed in the back twice by 29-year-old Winston Moseley, who later said his only motive was "to kill a woman". Moseley left the scene in his car. Genovese managed to crawl to the back of the building, but was blocked from entering by a closed door. Ten minutes passed until Moseley came back and eventually found Genovese lying in a hallway, barely conscious. It's almost unbearable to write this, but he stabbed her several times more before raping her. Knife wounds in Genovese's hands showed that she tried to defend herself as much as she could. Moseley fled away again, not to return this time. Genovese was found by a neighbor who called the police. Kitty Genovese died on her way to the hospital. The most tragic part of what expired is that there were several witnesses to at least parts of the ordeal that Genovese was put through by Moseley (who was soon caught and died in jail in 2016). The first newspaper article mentioned 38 witnesses, but that number has later been disputed. The fact remains that at least some people witnessed the first attack visually and shouted at the attacker, but did not intervene and did not even call the police. Genovese screamed several times and was heard by people in the neighborhood, but none responded. The response to this case was huge and resulted in the theory of the *bystander effect*, which has since been proven to be real by many experiments. The theory says that the more people are around when something tragic happens, the less likely someone is to intervene. This feels rather counterintuitive, since you would probably think that you'd be safer in an environment where lots of people are around.

Here is where I *must* insert the most personal paragraph of this book. In the year 2000, on a cold and rainy December Saturday night, or rather Sunday morning, I was walking to my car from an evening out in the city. There were several hundred people also walking to the nearby parking lots. Then my eye caught three men punching and kicking another man. I noticed the three men's clothing and recognized them to be neo-nazis – army boots, rolled up jeans, black bomber jackets, shaved heads, and some with nazi tattoos on their bald heads. The man being attacked was a black man in his forties. Hundreds of people must have noticed this awful scene. The black man was already unconscious as far as I could tell, but the neo-nazis kept kicking him. I felt anger boiling inside and – being a black belt taekwondo – I decided to step forward, towards the ugly scene. The three scumbags turned their attention towards me and started to curse and swear at me, asking me why I cared for a N-. I didn't say anything and just looked them in the eyes, being glad they stopped kicking the poor man. Remember, all this time, hundreds of people were passing by, making their way to their cars. Then I noticed four more figures stepping out of the shadows nearby. They turned out to be four more neo-nazis, bigger guys than the first three, as if these were the older brothers standing by, watching the younglings as they performed their disgusting act. The black man was still unconscious, while the now seven neo-nazis surrounded me. I had to make a quick decision here. Being a well-trained black belt, I figured I could probably take out four or five of these idiots, but maybe not all seven. What would they do to me if they would eventually prevail? Probably all I did to them, and add a little more. I also didn't know if they had knives on them, or even worse. Moreover, it was raining like hell and my shoes were pretty slippery. It must have been a split second, but in my mind it took ages before I finally decided to basically defend myself, but not to counterattack. My goal was to stop them from attacking the black man. The biggest neo-nazis grabbed me by my neck and both my arms from behind, while the smaller guys started kicking and punching like mad. One of them I remember the most – he had four seal rings around his right hand fingers and deliberately tried to punch in my teeth. But he didn't succeed. I was able to block most of the blows with my forehead and didn't feel much pain. Honestly, an average sparring game at taekwondo training was tougher than this. That only affirms that one trained fighter can do a whole lot more damage than seven untrained losers. After a few minutes of them pounding into me, the black man woke up. He started asking in blurry sentences why they did this to him, he hadn't done anything wrong, after all. Later, I found out he was a foreigner and a drifter who had no idea what neo-nazis were, and why they would hate him just for having a dark skin color. The result of his questions was that the dirtbags let me go and pointed their attention to him again. They again started kicking him, briefly this time, and then left the scene. I let them go and went to help the poor bastard who was in pain and heavily confused. This whole event lasted for about forty minutes in total. Hundreds and hundreds of people – young and fit – must have witnessed it. Nobody did a thing. What is even more excruciating, is that there always was a police van parked a couple of hundred meters down the road, with police officers watching people getting to their cars. Somebody could have simply gone up to them and told them, "hey, something's going on over there, you should have a look", but nobody did. Perhaps they all assumed someone else already did that. Perhaps no one wanted to get involved. Nevertheless, it was my own personal encounter with the *bystander effect* that I, of course, will never forget. There's two lessons I drew from this ordeal. One, never were slippery shoes when going out. Two, if I ever find myself in a similar situation, I will immediately, without delay, start fighting like hell – no holds barred. I had no idea at the time that their fighting would be so weak. Looking back, without slippery shoes, I could have taken out all seven of them in a matter of minutes. Hindsight is always 20/20, I guess.

In case you're wondering what to do if you get caught in a "bystander" situation, the best thing according to theory and experiments, is to physically point at bystanders and give them orders, like, "You! Call 911!", "You! Come pressure this wound!", et cetera. That will generally move people to act.

Back to business. In traditional organizations, managers appoint people to do certain work, which makes it hard for someone to *not* take responsibility, since it is forced upon you. In modern organizations with more focus on self-organization, there is a severe risk of falling victim to the *bystander effect*. If "the team" is responsible for a certain piece of work and "someone" from the team needs to pick up certain tasks, *who* is going to do that? Especially in beginning teams and in organizations in which a culture of hierarchy still prevails, it is common that people stay quietly on the sidelines, not picking up the work – avoiding "getting involved", avoiding personal responsibility, or simply forgetting to pick up work, because they are so much used to being told what to do. All the more reason to be very aware of the *bystander effect* in modern organizations.

The Prisoner's Dilemma

In social psychology, a small hypothetical story is used to point out a situation that occurs quite often in our daily lives, not in the least at work. The story goes as follows. Two bank robbers manage to steal a hefty sum of money from a bank and are able to hide the loot before the cops capture them both. The police don't have that much to go on, since they have the bank robbers, but not the money. The robbers are held for questioning in separate cells. Then the police questioner plays a devious game on them. Both are proposed that if they tell on their mate, and their mate does not, they go free immediately and their co-robber will be imprisoned for 20 years. If both tell on each other, their prison sentence will be short but substantial, 5 years. And if neither one turns their back on the other, the evidence is mostly circumstantial and they will both have to serve 1 year in prison. The *prisoner's dilemma* is then, will I cooperate with my friend, or will I defect and try and save my hide – with the risk attached that my friend does the same? What if I cooperate, and my friend defects? That would be really terrible! What are the odds? There is no real solution to this dilemma.

At work, you might encounter the *prisoner's dilemma* as a manager, for instance, when there is an organization overhaul taking place. When the budgets are to be (re-)distributed, do you go for what's good for the company, or do you go for what's good for your department? Do you cooperate with other managers, or do you defect and hope they won't do the same?

Tit-for-tat

A onetime *prisoner's dilemma* is a true nerve-wrecking predicament. Things change, however, if you face the same *prisoner's dilemma* over and over again. Think, for instance, of stakeholders of a product that you make. In a modern environment, you probably work in iterations – like *Scrum Sprints* of several weeks. Each new iteration, the stakeholders get to exert their influence on the backlog for the product. If they could express their desires only once, that would entail a *single prisoner's dilemma*, but now it has become an *iterated prisoner's dilemma*. What do you do in terms of cooperation or defection if you knew you would face the other parties involved in a couple of weeks' time again? Ukranian-American mathematical psychologist Anatol Rapoport (1911-2007) came up with an elegant and simple solution to the *iterated prisoner's dilemma* around 1980, taking part in the *Axelrod Tournaments*, which focused on *cooperation* and were highly influential on *game theory*. Rapoport's strategy is called *tit-for-tat* and works like a small computer program:

1. In the first round, cooperate.
2. In every next round, do whatever the other party did the previous round.

So, let's say, in the first round, you cooperate and the other party cooperates too, that means you will cooperate the second round as well. If the other party then defects, you will defect the third round – otherwise, cooperate again. The solution is elegant because it starts from a point of good will, but is no sucker if the other party is of ill will.

In case of the stakeholders at work, if they learn of this little elegant strategy called *tit-for-tat*, they might be inclined to start out in a cooperative mode, and mood. In a situation where resources are scarce, the willingness to cooperate and let others have a fair share of the work capacity will in the end be the best solution for the organization overall.

The Ultimatum Game

In the previous segment about the *tit-for-tat* solution to the *iterative prisoner's dilemma*, the so-called *game theory* is mentioned, which is the study of mathematical models of strategic interaction between *rational* decision-makers. *Game theory* saw the light of day in a 1928 proof written by Hungarian-American polymath John von Neumann (1903-1957) – considered by many to be the most intelligent person to ever have lived. In 1944, Von Neumann co-authored *Theory of Games and Economic Behavior* with German-American economist Oskar Morgenstern (1902-1977), which further lay the basis for the groundbreaking new field of *game theory*, used in a wide variety of sciences, from social science to computer science. As mentioned, game theory starts with the assumption of *rational* or *logical* decision-makers. The trouble is, that we are not as rational or logical as we think we are. The so-called *ultimatum game* is a prime example of that.

Consider the following narrative. Someone offers you ten dollars on one condition – the *ultimatum*. You have to share the ten dollars with a total stranger and the stranger has to agree with how you split the ten dollars between the two of you. Now, if we humans were purely rational actors, you should offer the stranger one dollar and keep nine dollars yourself. A purely rational stranger would consider that one dollar is more than zero dollars, so a good catch! But we all know that we – as the stranger – would feel this division to be unfair, knowing that the proposer would keep nine times as much money than they offer us. A more acceptable split would be five-five or perhaps four-six, but other than that would already feel weird.

You might think this irrational feeling of unfairness is solely human, but you'd be mistaken. Dutch primatologist and ethologist Frans de Waal (1948) has done a lot of research over the years on the behavior of apes and monkeys. One of his experiments involved giving one capuchin monkey a grape a few times in a row – which capuchins absolutely love –

while handing another monkey a piece of cucumber instead – which capuchins don't hate, but find not as delicious as grapes. The monkeys could see each other, and they could see what the other was receiving – a grape or a piece of cucumber. It turns out that after a few rounds of getting the not-so-delicious cucumber, that capuchin became really pissed off at the giver of the food, so much that the monkey throws the cucumber back at the experimenter. If the monkey had been purely rational, it would have been happy to receive any nutritious food, but to know that the neighbor is getting the sweeter grape is an unbearable unfairness. You can find the quite hilarious video of this experiment on the internet (search for "capuchin grape cucumber").

Researchers have even figured out that it actually pays off to be irrational in real life. If you, for instance, don't even agree with a five-five split, but demand six dollars – as the stranger – you will get a reputation of being difficult and hard-to-please, of being irrational. The next time someone wants to make a deal with you, they know they won't even have to try a four-six deal or worse, because they know you'll explode if you hear that. So, being a little irrational actually pays off in the long run, others will try and please you before you even know it.

Loss Aversion

Besides De Waal, there is another scientist carrying out experimental games with monkeys and other non-human animals – like dogs – and that is professor of psychology Laurie Santos (1975) of Yale University. She has done quite a few very intricate games with capuchins to see if their economic behavior matches our *irrational* human economic behavior. We've already seen that De Waal made capuchins angry by giving them pieces of cucumber instead of grapes, and Santos took things a step further. In one experiment, she had a colleague show a monkey *one* grape and then subsequently give him either one grape, or two grapes, at random. Another monkey was shown *two* grapes and then – again, at random – given either one or two grapes. So, to be clear about this, the end result was exactly the same for the monkeys – they were given either one or two grapes at random. The beginning was a different experience for them however, and the question was, does that matter? And the answer is yes. The game was played several rounds with numerous monkeys and the results were the same each time. The monkeys that were shown only one grape to start with, were fairly happy throughout the experiment. They were shown one, and sometimes got one, sometimes got two grapes, nice! But the other group was not so pleased. They were shown two, and sometimes got two, but also sometimes only one grape, not so nice! What's going on here? Why the grumpiness, if the end result is the same in both cases – either one or two grapes, at random. The answer is that this is a case of *loss aversion* – which was described by Nobel Prize winner Daniel Kahneman in his so-called *prospect theory*.

We've already run into Daniel Kahneman in the previous chapter, once on *Thinking Fast & Slow*, and once on *Heuristics & Biases*, and now we meet Kahneman and his colleague Amos Tversky again, in light of the *prospect theory*, which they developed in 1979. The basic premise of the theory is that the prospect of *losing* 10 dollars feels *much worse* than the prospect of *gaining* 10 dollars feels *good*. Hence the concept of *loss aversion* – we have an aversion to losing something we already have, much more so than an appetite for getting something we want but don't have yet, even if we don't have things physically in our hands but only see them the effect already takes place.

Back to professor Santos and the capuchins, because they did some more tests in relation to *loss aversion*. One experiment went like this – and bear with me, this is tricky to keep track of.

Grape salesman A shows the monkeys *one* grape and then – when the monkey gives a token – he *always* gives the monkey *two* grapes.

Grape salesman B also shows *one* grape, but then gives the monkey either *one* grape or *three* grapes. In other words, from the monkey's perspective, this guy is more riskier to give the token to, because you could end up with only one grape instead of the sure two grapes you'll get from A.

As it turns out, monkeys are risk aversive in this experiment and prefer salesman A over salesman B – they would rather have the sure 2 grapes. But now for the second part of this experiment.

Grape salesman C shows the monkeys *three* grapes and always gives them *two* grapes.

Grape salesman D also shows *three* grapes, but then gives the monkey either *three* grapes or only *one* grape.

Now, the monkeys show *irrational* behavior. They now prefer salesman D over salesman C, apparently trying to *avoid the loss* of grapes given. They would rather take the risky chance of *maybe* getting the three grapes over the *sure* loss of one grape with salesman C. This is exactly what *loss aversion* is.

Does this relate to human behavior, you might wonder, and the answer is a full-blown yes. We humans show the exact same *irrational* economic behavior in real life. Instead of grapes, you could use money to illustrate the same behavior with humans. Let's say you have 100 dollars and if you give person A 10 dollars, A will always give you 20 dollars back. If you give person B 10 dollars, he will sometimes give you back your 10 dollars, sometimes 20 bucks. If you're allowed to give either A or B 10 dollars a few times in a row, most people will choose A every time, since he's a sure bet – your wealth will absolutely surely accumulate. We generally find B too risky – we might end up with the same we started with. But if we switch things around again, like with the capuchins, our attitude changes. Let's again say you start with 100 dollars. If you give person C 10 dollars, they will surely take the 10 dollars. If you give person D 10 dollars, they will sometimes return your 10, but sometimes grab 20 dollars instead. As we saw with the monkeys, in this case, we turn irrational all of a sudden and most will actually prefer person D – since there is a good chance that we are able to hold on to our money every round and end up with exactly what we started with. We don't want to part with our dear money so easily. We are aversive to loss.

The money case described above is quite simplistic, but if you make it more complicated, like, for instance, make it a stock exchange, then things get really complicated fast. The thing is, the *loss aversion* still applies, no matter how complicated the system. This is exactly the reason for people holding on to plummeting stocks and bonds for way too long, resulting in bigger losses than necessary from a rational point of view. People hate to part with what they have in their possession and somehow hope – irrationally – that they can hold on to assets that *could* become worth more again, but are in fact becoming worth less and less.

How does *loss aversion* relate to our modern work environments then? One thing I've seen in so many organizations is the use of *stretched goals*. You will encounter them in traditional project management projects – with *Stretched Project Goals*, but also in Agile environments – with *Stretched Sprint Goals*, or *Stretched Program Increment Objectives*. What it basically comes down to is, we have a certain main goal set, but if we reach that goal and happen to have extra time and resources available, we'll go for the stretched goal and try to reach that too. From experience, I can say, that rarely happens.

What you've done then, when you've told your stakeholders up-front about the *stretched goal*, is that you've shown your stakeholders *two* grapes, and ended up giving them only one. We saw what happened with the capuchins – they got pretty upset after several rounds of that, whereas the monkeys that were always shown one grape and sometimes given two grapes, were happy as a clam. The same holds true for your stakeholders. If you reach your Sprint Goals every two weeks, but rarely your Stretched Goals, your stakeholders are going to get grumpy – they won't be able to help themselves. Even though, rationally speaking, they always get good value from your team, they feel like they're missing out on something – they "lose" the value of the Stretched Goal every two weeks.

Only tell your stakeholders about your one main goal. Your aim is to reach that one main goal all the time – every sprint, every project, every program increment, et cetera. *If* you can find time and resources to do something extra after you've already reached your main goal, then by all means, try and reach a secondary goal that you figure out on the spot (the most valuable to complete as soon as possible). If you also manage to reach that secondary goal, imagine the surprise and happiness of your stakeholders when you present them the result. Never use Stretched Goals, avoid the *loss aversion*.

Chapter Four – Therapy as Coaching

There are quite a few similarities between being a coach and being a therapist. The surroundings may differ – an office building instead of a therapist's office – but the actual day to day work often falls into the same category, namely, helping people overcome obstacles so they can move ahead, feeling fitter, performing better. Psychological therapists face the daunting task of guiding their clients to better ways of dealing with issues and to a better way of life in general. They use different tools to accomplish permanent changes in the lives of their clients and in this chapter we're going to see how some of these tools might also be of help to coaches who work to effectuate lasting change in organizations.

Team Coaching

While it may be easy to assume a business coach usually helps with practical work-related issues at hand, and not – like the therapist – with personal obstacles that not necessarily have something to do with the workplace, in practice, the opposite is often true. More often than not, the work-related issues have their roots in the *thinking* and *behavior* of the individual employees, thus relating to their personal inner psychological life.

From my personal experience I can honestly say that the more I have been coaching teams, departments, and organizations, the more I've realized that it mostly comes down to coaching *individuals* in those teams, departments, and organizations. This realization runs counter to much of what you read online in social media and in articles in magazines, where there is a constant focus on *team coaching*. There are many theories out in the field about *coaching teams*, from the *Five Dysfunctions of a Team* by Patrick Lencioni (as discussed in the previous chapter, in the segment about *reference groups*), to the heavily quoted American psychological researcher Bruce Tuckman (1938-2016), who brought us his *Stages of Group Development*.

Tuckman

In 1965, Tuckman named four phases of group development: *Forming*, *Storming*, *Norming*, and *Performing*. And in 1977, he added a fifth phase, called *Adjourning*. When a team is put together, it starts in the *Forming* phase, in which team members are cautiously finding their place in the team. When the team has been together for a while and the first tentative positions are taken, various opinions and characters will start to butt heads, causing the *Storming* phase. When the dust settles, and the team members come to mutual agreed upon rules and regulations, the team enters the *Norming* phase. After that, the team members know each other fully well, and they know what to expect from one another. Having the guard rails – the norms – in place, they will enter the *Performing* phase. Great teams will thus reach the *Valhalla* of team levels, they will become a *High-Performance* team (sometimes also called a *High-Performing* team). The fifth phase that Tuckman added is the dismantling of the team, when each team member goes their own way.

Lately, there has been some criticism of Tuckman's phases. In real life, we seldom see teams going through (all) phases, and certainly not in this order – often going back and forth between phases, skipping phases, or seemingly in a phase that was not mentioned in Tuckman's model. From personal experience I can say that when I'm hired as a coach to (also) coach teams, many teams I encounter are bouncing around between *Storming, Norming,* and *Performing* all the time. The most difficult teams are the teams that seem to be in the *Performing* phase, but are not exactly *High-Performance* teams. Then it's up to me to see how they can improve to become a *High-Performance* team.

Whatever stands from Lencioni's and Tuckman's theories, you can tell from these ideas about *group dynamics* that bringing teams to a higher performance level involves a lot of psychological work, next to any technical elevation that might be needed. In my earlier days, when I was asked to raise a team to higher levels, I sought refuge in theories and best practices around *teams* – like Lencioni and Tuckman. And I also tried fitting different personalities together, based on, for instance, personality types derived from DISC or Myer-Briggs (see the first chapter for the debunking of these popular personality assessments), or the nine team roles from Belbin.

Belbin

English researcher and management consultant Raymond Meredith Belbin (1926) based his model on the success of teams on eight – later nine – different *team roles* he deducted from his observations and experience as a management consultant. His advice was to always make sure every one of the roles could be carried out by a member of a (management) team. This needn't be a different person per role, one team member can also carry out several "Belbin roles". The roles he described were the following:

1. The *Plant* – a clever, creative, independent thinker, but not so good on the communication

front; the term is somewhat misleading, by the way – Belbin said he called this role *plant* because one of his clients insisted they *plant* one of these in each group.

2. The *Resource Investigator* – a networker with a focus outside the team, great to have around at the start, but tends to forget to follow things through.

3. The *Co-ordinator* – a stable and mature delegator who is able to see the big picture, but can be perceived as manipulative and tends to delegate *too* much.

4. The *Shaper* – a task-focused extravert who likes challenging the team in order to improve and, ultimately, win; can become aggressive and bad-humored.

5. The *Monitor Evaluator* – a logical analyst who is able to observe with little bias and comes to proper decisions, but who can be too critical, and less passionate than others.

6. The *Teamworker* – a good listener and diplomat, good at solving conflicts; their (positive) influence might go unnoticed and their impartiality might cause indecisiveness.

7. The *Implementer* – an efficient and self-disciplined planner, who may be considered closed-minded and inflexible.

8. The *Completer Finisher* – a perfectionist with a knack for accuracy who will make sure everything is in order; might worry excessively about minor details and is not a good delegator.

9. The *Specialist* – this late addition to the Belbin roles is a highly skilled and knowledgeable person who loves to share that knowledge, but who is only interested in their narrow slice of expertise.

To determine what role – or which roles – would fit a person best, there are tests you can take – these days also online. The *Belbin Team Inventory* test – or the *Belbin Self-Perception Inventory* test, or the *Belbin Team Role Inventory* test – assesses an individual's behavior, based on both self-assessment and 360 degree feedback from colleagues. Belbin himself has always maintained that the roles are not like the DISC or Myers-Briggs personality types, and that the test is not a psychometric instrument. He invented his model in the first place to inform management consulting practices. The most important conclusion was that the best teams are teams that are balanced in the sense that all roles are represented in the team. Like mentioned, not every role has to be fulfilled by a different team member. As a matter of fact, Belbin claimed that the optimum team size is *four*, which would entail that each team member takes on multiple roles.

As much as these team coaching tools are at times helpful, they stop short of addressing individual coaching, which – in my opinion – is what *real* change usually comes down to. Just like real change in society starts with personal, individual change, so does real change in organizations only happen thoroughly when individuals change their thinking and behavior. In the end, the collective of all individuals together actually forms the organization. The same can be said for a team. The individual team members together shape the team itself.

The Coach as a Therapist

Considering that true organizational change happens only when (certain) individuals within the organization change their thinking and behavior, it makes sense to explore the tools that psychotherapists use to bring about change in their clients' behavior and reasoning.

Before we dive into the world of psychotherapy, I want to set some expectations. When we talk about *therapy*, what are we actually talking about? I suspect that many of you picture a client, slash patient, lying on a couch, with a serious-looking grey-haired gentleman with spectacles sitting right next to the couch, one leg over the other, in a comfortable armchair – near the head of the client – sporting a pen and a notepad, asking serious questions. These questions could range from, "how are we feeling today?", to, "when I say *gun*, you say…" This would be the image of classical psychotherapy in the era of Freud.

Psychodynamic psychotherapy

Austrian neurologist Sigmund Freud (1856-1939) founded what is known as *psychodynamic psychotherapy*, basically what is described in the paragraph above – a dialogue between a patient and a therapist, in which the therapist takes the lead and guides the patient. Freud named his theories and methods *psychoanalysis*. Today, the term *psychoanalysis* is used for forms of *psychodynamic psychotherapy* that closely align with Freud's methods – in practice only about 10% of therapists use the term. Therapies which are more loosely based on Freud's methods are called *psychodynamic therapy* – around 15% of therapists consider themselves to fall into this category.

Some characteristics of *psychodynamic psychotherapy* include a focus on the *unconscious*, finding clues about personal issues in early childhood experiences, finding meaning in a patients' specific use of words – including mistakes, and dissecting dreams to find clues to the unconscious. The therapist – the *psychoanalyst* in Freud's lingo – searches for gateways into the unconscious of the patient and derives meaning from what is found. Thus, by relaying these findings to the patient through questioning, the analyst makes the patient aware of their unconscious thoughts, which helps them to act upon these now conscious thoughts. Conflicting beliefs can be sorted out and unrealistic beliefs and pursuits can be realigned to more healthy thoughts. It is essential for the patient to experience these insights themselves, and not just have the analyst explain them to them.

Humanistic psychotherapy

In 1951, American psychologist Carl Rogers (1902-1987) introduced what he called *client-centered therapy*. Rogers took a different approach from Freud to the therapeutic process and focused not on the ability of the therapist (the psychoanalyst) to find meaning in the words of the patient, but rather on the ability of the client to gain insights into their own thoughts and words. Modern therapists who adhere to this method speak of a *person-based therapy*, in which the therapist and the client explore the inner world of the client *together*. Key to this approach is the respectful and supportive manner in which the therapist handles the process with the client, in which the client is allowed to take the lead and the therapist minds their own thoughts and words carefully in order to be fully empathic and unconditionally supporting towards the client.

These "classic" forms of psychotherapy are usually quite extensive in nature. They sometimes require multiple sessions per week and can run from anywhere between a few months to several years. As you might imagine, these forms of therapy are a little less suited for a work environment. Nonetheless, as a coach in an organization built up of individuals, it might at times be effective to apply some of these psychodynamic techniques to get to the nitty-gritty of a certain person's character and issues in order to force a breakthrough in a tough situation. I have certainly initiated my share of one-on-one conversations with persons that were blocking the progress of a team or even an entire department. I've always tried to use the more humanistic approach, to be empathic and a careful listener, asking triggering questions to try and guide someone to new understandings. I've had people break down and cry in front of me more than once. Even though one can be blind to their own behavior, I'd like to think the tears were not the result of my brutishness, but rather of the person's own illuminating insights into their thoughts and behavior – but who knows.

Cognitive Behavioral Therapy

Au contraire to the psychodynamic approach, the behavioral and cognitive therapies focus on the observable symptoms a client displays, rather than on the supposedly underlying issues that cause certain symptoms. Let's say when you get gloomy, you start to eat too much. A psychodynamic therapist would try and find out why you start eating too much when you get gloomy. This therapist would try to find the root cause of your problem and make you stop reaching for food by making you fully aware of your underlying issues. If you know and understand your unconscious desire to raid the fridge, then you can consciously stop yourself in your tracks. A cognitive behavioral therapist wouldn't spend time and effort on finding the deeper reasons why, they would simply try and stop you in your tracks before raiding the fridge. They would try to create a new and better environment for you in order for you to be able to adopt healthier habits instead.

One common feature of both behavioral and cognitive therapies is the use of *metrics* – measuring and recording the data by writing it down is an integral part of the process. The data will then show if the therapy is working or not.

Behavior Therapy

If we look strictly at *behavior therapy*, then this form of therapy is closely related to *classical conditioning*. In chapter six, about the history of psychology, we will learn more about *conditioning*, but for now, it suffices to say that in a conditioning process, an individual is being taught to behave in a certain way by providing a stimulus in that direction – in simpler words, given a reward for desired behavior (and perhaps punishment for undesired behavior).

Contingency management

Therapy based on changing the relationship between behavior and reward is called *contingency management*. In case of the unhealthy eating habit, which provides a temporary feeling of satisfaction, a therapist might work with the client to pick up physical exercise instead. If the client feels the need to raid the fridge, they should do ten push-ups first. Just by doing that, certain hormones are released and a satisfactory feeling will be triggered, thus lowering the felt need to raid the fridge. By doing exercises, the person will also feel better about themselves, and eventually, will also *see* that they're doing better – in the mirror. The altered contingency between behavior and reward results in a lasting behavioral change.

How could we use behavioral therapy techniques at work? For instance, if someone has a habit of becoming angry at the office, a behavior therapist will wonder, what's in it for this person to behave this way? What reward does this individual receive that stimulates them to continue this unhealthy behavior? Perhaps the scared looks on the faces of their colleagues makes them feel powerful, or perhaps the anger prevents others from asking difficult questions. As a coach, you will then look for alternative rewards for healthier behavior. You could ask the other team members to express praise to their team mate if they behave friendly or smile. Thus, the person will experience this new reward when displaying the desired behavior. The satisfactory feeling (the praise) will only enforce this behavior more.

Exposure treatment

Behavior therapy has a strong track record when it comes to treating phobias, like fearing spiders. What therapists do is expose a client to a mild and more distant specimen of something they fear, for instance spiders. They might first show a *drawing* of a spider, see if the individual can hold it together. Then – if successful – the therapist might show a picture of a spider, then a video of a moving spider, and so on, until the client can stomach holding a live tarantula on their hand. Despite its relative success, only about 10% of therapists describe themselves as behavioral therapist.

On the work floor you could apply this approach with a team that feels hesitant to adopt Scrum. You can expose them to small changes first, like introducing a daily fifteen minute scrum. Once they get used to that – which process is called *habituation* – initiate a retrospective once every two weeks, and thus, slowly take away their fear of Agile methods by gradually exposing them to the real thing.

Cognitive Therapy

Right next to the *behavioral therapy* there is *cognitive therapy*. Where behavior therapy immediately starts with adapting one's behavior, cognitive therapy first tries to make you *think* differently. Think of a behavior therapist as a *trainer* and of a cognitive therapist as a *teacher*. The basic idea behind cognitive therapy is that rational thoughts of the client can overcome the irrational beliefs of that same client. Therapists will "force" clients to think from different angles by asking many questions or by stating observations that contradict the beliefs of the client.

ABC theory of emotions

American psychologist Albert Ellis (1913-2007) fell out of love with psychodynamic therapy in the 1950s. Instead of the elaborate therapy, Ellis introduced his now widely used *ABC theory of emotions* – in which the A stands for *Activating event*, B for *Belief*, and C for *Consequent emotion*. With that, Ellis meant that the client was at one point triggered by an *Activating event* to a certain *Belief*, that led to a *Consequent emotion*. For instance, one of your colleagues said "hi!" to another colleague this morning in the hallway on the way up to the coffee machine, but the " hi!" was not returned. Your colleague now has the belief that nobody likes them at work and is therefore sad and a bit angry. The saying hi and the subsequent not returning of the hi is the *Activating event*. The *Belief* is that nobody likes them, and the sadness and anger are the *Consequent emotions*.

The therapist will now address the irrational belief that "nobody likes them" by disputing that belief. Ellis was one to ridicule irrational beliefs with a sense of humor. He might have told our colleague to stop "awfulizing" – to stop making things worse than they truly are. One could question if the other colleague even heard the "hi", or if they were sunken in thoughts instead. Or, *even* if this one colleague truly didn't like them, that wouldn't mean "nobody" liked them. The disputation by the therapist would eventually have to lead to a new belief in our client, namely that it is actually not the case that "nobody likes them". Some have extended the ABC of Ellis to ABCDE, with the D standing for the *Disputation*, and the E for the *Effective new belief.*

Even though the therapist goes against the irrational belief of the client, the cognitive therapist will do so from an empathic and caring point of view, more in line with the humanistic therapy approach than with the psychoanalytic approach. Hence Ellis' use of humor to dispute the irrational belief.

Having had this one time insight and new belief is not the end of the therapy. The second phase takes longer and is more difficult. To replace long-held erroneous ideas with more healthy thoughts, the client is often given homework. Where psychodynamic psychotherapy is mostly done in the therapist's office, cognitive therapy moves from office to the client's environment. The client might receive homework in the form of keeping a sort of diary in which they would have to write down any irrational thoughts they have during the day, and what might be a more healthy thought instead. Thus, the client makes themselves aware of the better, healthier alternatives, needing less and less help from the therapist. The role of the therapist in this phase slowly transforms from that of being a teacher to being more of a coach. The frequency of meetings will go down and will – eventually – not be necessary anymore, when the client has gained the upper hand on the irrational thoughts.

This direct and thought-based therapeutic approach is very usable in an office environment. If I, as an Agile Coach, encounter a manager who has very old-fashioned ideas about running a department – very Theory X – then I need to be aware of Activating events happening to which the manager will respond with a certain belief and feel certain emotions about. If, for instance, new unexpected work is coming in (*Activating event*), the manager might believe (*Belief*) that they must estimate the size of the work and divide the work over their teams, feeling irritated (*Consequent emotions*) by this new work forcing them to replan what was carefully planned out by them up-front. I can then dispute the belief that the manager has to estimate the size of the work and that they have to divide the work over the teams. I can ask why the teams cannot do that themselves. I can suggest having a few people from different teams quickly have a look at the inbound work and have them assess which team would be best to pick this up. Once decided on the team, I will suggest to have that team estimate how much work it actually is, in their eyes. Once we know that, we can make a proper decision about when we should do this work. In an Agile environment, I would insist the Product Owner of that team would take the lead on that decision. Thus, the estimate of the work will be much more realistic, the prioritization of the work will be healthier – business wise, and the role of the manager in this process would have been minimized almost entirely, diminishing a lot of stress for both the manager and the rest of the department. Everytime unexpected work comes in, I – as a coach – will step in and confront the irrational beliefs of the manager, until the day comes when the manager themselves will say, I don't need to worry about this, I'll take this to the teams. Then my work – in that area – is done. The biggest difference with the therapy is that it is a bit harder to give people homework in a work environment, but in some cases, that might even be applicable.

Socratic questioning

Around the same time that Albert Ellis lost interest in *psychodynamic therapy*, American psychiatrist Aaron Beck (1921) followed a similar path. Beck is considered to be the father of both *cognitive therapy* and *cognitive behavioral therapy*, and overall seen as the most influential of all cognitive therapists. Where Ellis could be considered a bit blunt because of his use of humor – which not everyone might be amused by – Beck uses the gentler approach of merely asking questions. These questions, however, are just as leading as Ellis' disputations. The technique used by Beck is known as *Socratic Questioning*. The questions the therapist asks the client are open questions – so not questions to which you can simply answer a "yes" or a "no" – and they are "powerful" questions, on which the client has to ponder a bit before being able to answer. *Powerful questions* often start with "what", "who", "where", "when", or "why". For instance, instead of asking the weaker question, "do you like working in this team?", you could ask, "what do you like about working in this team?" Here are some more examples of powerful questions:

- What could you do right now to improve the situation?
- What would be the first step towards your goal?
- What would be the best next step for the team to take?
- Where do you fear we end up if nothing changes?
- What is the worst that could happen if we take this route?
- What would we do if we had no obstacles and unlimited resources available?
- What's missing from this conversation?
- What are you seeing happening right now?
- How would it make you feel if we succeeded with this plan?
- Win or lose, what would you like to learn from this experience?
- If we're saying "yes" to this, what are we saying "no" to?

Beck's approach also makes use of homework for the client, similar to Ellis' approach – writing down irrational or dysfunctional thoughts and describing healthier ideas instead. The fact that *cognitive behavioral therapy* is utilized in cases of severe depression and *borderline personality disorder*, tells us of its powerfulness. This is a good reason to include *Socratic Questioning* in your bag of tricks. Its power – when applied well – is enormous, also in corporate environments. The only issue is its difficulty of mastering. It's not easy to ask powerful questions. In practice, people tend to slip into asking *closed* questions much easier. Often, the coach already has an idea of where to go – or so they assume – which results in asking questions that are "leading the witness". It takes a lot of practice – in real-life situations – to be able to apply *Socratic Questioning* in a powerful manner. But once mastered, it could be the most powerful tool in your toolbox. I have encountered other coaches that were so strong with this technique, it was almost scary. You would know up-front, whatever sort of meeting it was, if they were there, they would be sitting silently in a corner – brooding on the question and the moment to ask it – and then, when people least expected it, there they were, asking this one stupefying question that left the whole room speechless and some – like me – with a slight smile on their face, knowing that we were all, once again, outwitted by the powerful questioner that made us all rethink our irrational approach.

Does Therapy Work?

Talking about these different forms of therapy almost makes you forget one very important question that the scientific inquisitive mind should be asking – *does therapy even work?*

Ever since the days of Freud, the number of therapies has skyrocketed. About 5% of the therapists describe themselves as psychodynamic – thus at least loosely basing their therapy on Freud's methods. Almost 30% think of themselves as cognitive therapists, and another 30% of the therapists consider themselves *eclectic* – meaning, they use a mixture of all kinds of therapies. These days, you can find numerous new forms of therapy, ranging from "running therapy" to "mindfulness based cognitive therapy". What numerous studies over the years have shown is that around 60% of psychotherapy clients feel better after a certain period of time – think months here. That sounds like a good piece of evidence vouching *for* therapy. There are a few caveats, however. First of all, control studies show that about 30% of the people who are on a waiting list to become a therapy client *also* feel better after a period of time. This means that out of the 60% of the clients that feel better after a while, half of them would have felt better even if they hadn't received the therapy. This leaves only 30% that feel better because of the therapy. Another caveat is that it does matter *which* form of therapy is used – not all therapies are created equal. Also, what works for one, might not work for another, and vice versa. What seems to help in most cases is two things – a good relationship between the client and the therapist, and the amount of trust that the client has in the form of therapy being right for them.

Do these low numbers indicate that you shouldn't even consider therapy if you suffer mentally? No, that it does not. As a matter of fact, *physical healthcare* shows similar scores on effectiveness, so *mental healthcare* is not out of step in that respect. What you *do* need to do – and this applies to the use of therapeutic tools in a business environment as well – is to set your expectations. You cannot expect these techniques to be wondertools that will bend wills or heal souls with a snap of your fingers. Life's never that easy.

Positive Psychology

On a more positive note – pun intended – there's this thing called *Positive Psychology*. You can see the term popping up in social media left and right, but it is often either misused or misinterpreted.

American psychologist Martin Seligman (1942) is the father of *Positive Psychology*. What he noticed was that psychology has always been about helping out and dealing with people who were somehow mentally deficient – there was something wrong with them. Seligman took into consideration that this is only a small percentage of the entire population and thought about all those other people that are mentally normal and healthy. He wondered what psychology could do for them. This gave birth to *Positive Psychology*. The name itself is often misunderstood – it is not about being positive all the time and getting rid of gloomy feelings. The name is derived from the idea that people with psychological disorders need help to get from a subzero state to a zero baseline. *Positive Psychology* focuses instead on helping people rise from the baseline upwards – into the positive.

Seligman had thus entered new markets, much bigger markets than those of people with disorders. That's probably one of the main reasons for the rise in popularity of *Positive Psychology* over the last few decades. Even though the results achieved with *Positive Psychology* are significant – meaning, they make a *noticeable* difference, albeit rather small – one should be careful out in the wild about adopting methods and ideas that from the surface seem to be related to *Positive Psychology*, but are rather part of the "toxic positivity" scene that was mentioned in the first chapter.

Sport Psychology

If you take the positive even further upwards, you enter the realm of *high-performance*. One of the fields interested in high-performance is of course *sports*. Where sports used to focus entirely on the physical prowess of athletes, it nowadays takes the psychology behind sports achievements very seriously. Even though the first careful sport psychology was already conducted in the 1920s, in the last few decades it has really taken a flight. Sport psychology focuses – amongst other aspects – on motivation, dealing with stress and anxiety, and finding the right state of mind for optimal performance. Techniques that sport psychologists and coaches use include *goal setting*, *visualization*, and *self-talk*.

Coaches in business environments would be smart to borrow some of these same techniques and ideas to lift their teams into the realms of high-performance. Take for instance the goal setting. A lot has to do with applying the right *metrics*. If you set measurable goals, you can work towards achieving them, which gives you a good feeling if you reach them, and always leaves room for improvement – because once you have reached a goal, you set the bar higher. What is very useful to learn from sport psychology is the identification of different sorts of goals. For instance, a marathon runner might aim for a win at the New York marathon next year. That would be an *outcome metric* – do they win or not? The same runner might also work – during the year of training towards the New York marathon – on setting a personal record every two months. That would be a *performance metric*. The runner might at the same time be working on improving the way they place their feet on the concrete, or on improving eating habits, or sleep rhythm. These improvements would fall under the category of *process metrics*.

If you coach a team, *outcome metrics* would measure profit, cost-reduction, or an increase in the *Net Promoter Score*. *Performance metrics* would measure the number of releases of software in a year, the number of production incidents in a month, or the percentage of tests that are automated. *Process metrics* would focus on, for instance, team happiness, team skill balance, or the communication skill level.

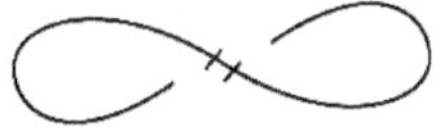

Chapter Five – What's Next?

We've already seen how proven psychological insights can be of great help in our modern work environments today. In this chapter, we'll explore what psychology might bring to the future of our organizations.

Morality

Modern organizations feel a growing need to not just satisfy the monetary gains of owners, stakeholders, and employees. In general, people are becoming more aware of aspects like gender equality, racial equality, environmental footprints, animal rights, et cetera. This entails the need for a *moral compass* of an organization. The issue with morality is that different people adhere to different viewpoints they consider to be moral. In a large organization, you have to deal with not just the moral viewpoint of the leadership, but also of the employees, and of stakeholders. As we've seen in recent years, especially employees of modern, Agile-minded organizations like Facebook and Google have not taken this *moral compass* lightly.

In 2018, huge numbers of Google employees participated in the *Google Walkouts*, in which they literally walked out of the office building and demanded concrete changes from the company, including a commitment to end pay inequality, a transparent sexual harassment report, an inclusive process for reporting sexual misconduct, and to elevate the *Chief of Diversity* to answer directly to the CEO and create an *Employee Representative*. Some – but not all – demands have been met since then, but managers of large organizations in general were warned that their morality was on the table for all to see.

Also in 2018, Facebook employees were reportedly quitting or asking to switch departments over ethical concerns around the *Cambridge Analytica* scandal, in which a data-analytics company used information from millions of profiles to influence American voters during the 2016 presidential elections. Many of the employees believed their company could – and should – have done more to handle user data responsibly and were frustrated that CEO Mark Zuckerberg was silent for days after the allegations surfaced. A product designer was quoted as literally saying, "Morally, it was extremely difficult to continue working there."

In 2020, Facebook CEO Mark Zuckerberg again faced frustrated and outright angry employees, trying to explain his inaction on outrageous posts made by

American President Trump. Facebook employees staged a virtual walkout and in a direct conversation with Zuckerberg vented their moral anger. The top question for Zuckerberg, which called for changes to the company's stance on political speech, received more than 5,400 votes from workers, according to an employee that was present at the virtual conversation.

Later in 2020, after the horrible murder of George Floyd by the knee of a Minneapolis police officer, an Instagram employee (which is part of Facebook), tweeted that she was deeply disappointed and ashamed with how the company was responding to the worldwide *Black Lives Matter* movement. Even the Facebook director of product management added that, "I work at Facebook and I am not proud of how we're showing up. The majority of coworkers I've spoken to feel the same way. We are making our voice heard." In a personal Facebook post, CEO Zuckerberg publicly admitted that "Facebook needs to do more to support equality and safety for the Black community through our platforms."

Even though morality may mean different things to people from different walks of life, there is a psychological basis which is interesting in this respect. However much morality is often hijacked by the religious, who claim morality comes from their god(s) or their religion, studies have shown that there is little evidence for a moral effect of religious beliefs. Rather, research has shown that we are more likely to have been born with an innate sense of morality.

Canadian-American psychologist Paul Bloom (1963) has done a lot of interesting psychological experiments on morality with children too young to be affected by religion or other supposed moral institutions. In his 2013 book *Just Babies*, he describes some of these experiments that show a moral awareness in kids as young as six months old. In one such an experiment, a baby is shown two puppets. One of the puppets has a ball and plays with it. Then it hands over the ball to the other puppet, which takes the ball and makes a run for it – not such a nice move from this puppet. After this little stage play, the baby is handed both puppets to play with. In overwhelming numbers, the babies prefer the first puppet to the puppet that took the ball and ran. Now, if the babies would have had no sense of morality, they wouldn't have cared if the puppet played nice or not, but they *do* care, which shows a sense of what is right and what is wrong at even this young an age.

In chapter three we already saw – in the segment about the *Ultimatum Game* – that primatologist Frans De Waal found that capuchin monkeys also have a profound sense of fairness, which shows that morality is not solely a human thing either.

Artificial Intelligence

Speaking of non-humans, one of the conundrums we will face more and more, is the programming of *Artificial Intelligence. Bot programming* is already a hot topic in many large organizations. Keeping up a human servicedesk for customers is often an expensive matter which companies like to automate as soon as possible. These *bots* – short for *robots* – "know" what to answer when a customer enters a question. Only a couple of years ago, these bots were not much more than the FAQ-page (Frequently Asked Questions webpage) in the format of a simple conversation. Nowadays, many of these bots pose as real humans and they sometimes get away with it too. As a matter of fact, many online servicedesk chats start out with a bot and gradually go over into a conversation with a real human when the talk becomes too difficult for the bot to maintain. It is often hard to tell where the bot ended and the human started in such online (typed) conversations.

In the future, these bots will get more and more sophisticated and more humanlike in their conversations. If you're programming these bots and their conversational algorithms, you have to consider morality at some point. If you're programming health-care related bots, the conversations can become very private and delicate in nature. If you're programming bots for a dating app, you might be taking advantage of heartfelt feelings of others towards someone who doesn't really exist. Where do you draw the line? Of course that is first and foremost a question for the owner of the bot, the person who has the ultimate say over what the bot will act like, but what about your own moral sense? Will you just program anything they ask of you, or do you draw a line in the sand? And what if you're coaching a team that develops such bots and you feel a line is being crossed, do you draw attention to that, or do you leave it to the team and the business owner?

In the near future – and for some perhaps already current – we will need conversations about morality at work. Some of that conversation will no doubt wander into the realm of philosophy rather than psychology, but it pays off to understand the psychological origins of morality. Most psychologists consider morality a product of human evolution. When we were trying to survive on the plains of Africa – amongst many deadly predators – it paid off for humans to work together. If you start living together in a social structure, such as a tribe, it helps if you can trust the rest of the group. We've seen in chapter three – about the self and others – how important it is to feel accepted and respected by the group. If you share the same ideas about what is right and what is wrong, that puts your mind at ease and allows for the group members to let their guard down and spend time and energy on making progress for the entire tribe. People in those days with lower standards for what is right and what is wrong would have had more trouble assimilating in a tribe, and would therefore have had much worse opportunities to reproduce. From an evolutionary perspective, that would result in less a-social genes and more "moral" genes being spread. Over time, the human population was thus gradually equiped with a high sense of morality. For many other species who prefer living in groups, the very same principle applies.

The Trolley Problem and Self-driving cars

Bots are not likely to kill people in a conversation – even though we need to be careful with putting bots on emergency calls and on suicide-hotlines. But, there are other situations in which morality kicks in, in high gear. For instance, what if you're working on self-driving cars? That's a whole different ballgame altogether. To give some context around the issues at play, first a description of the much-used allegory called the *Trolley Problem*, introduced in 1967 by English philosopher Phillipa Foot (1920-2010).

Imagine the following situation. A trolley car is speeding down the tracks and its breaks seem to be malfunctioning. Up ahead are five people working on the tracks and if they don't move, they are going to get run over by the trolley-car, probably getting killed. There's a switch right in front of you, and if you pull the lever, the trolley is going to be diverted to another track. There is one catch though. On the other track, there is one worker who is not following the situation either, and that person will be run over and killed if you pull the lever. What do you do? Pull the lever or not? Let five innocent people be killed if you do nothing, or let innocent person be killed if you pull the lever? If you put this dilemma forward to people, most will say they would pull the lever and have one innocent life be taken, instead of five. In general, that seems to be the most moral choice.

What now if we change the circumstances a little bit? Let's assume the same basic beginning – a runaway trolley car is hurtling towards five innocent track workers. If nothing is done, five innocent lives are taken. Here comes the twist. There is a pedestrain bridge over the tracks, and you're standing on it, together with a very, very fat person. As a matter of fact, if you would push this morbidly obese person over the railing, their big fat body would surely cause the trolley car to derail, and thus save the five innocent track workers. Would you push the corpulent person over the edge, or not? The end results are the same – if you do nothing, five innocent lives are lost, if you do something, only one innocent life is lost. When *this* dilemma is put forward to people, most will choose *not* to push the voluminous person in front of the trolley car. Somehow this is different for most people. Apparently, pulling a lever from a distance of the drama is much easier than actually physically touching and partaking in the drama.

Back to the self-driving cars. What if you have to program the algorithm that kicks in when a form of the trolley problem arises? What if you have to program what to do when the car finds itself in a situation in which it simply cannot avoid causing a collision with a person? Let's say the car sees two elderly people crossing the street all of a sudden to the left, and a mother with a baby carriage to the right. The car is slipping and going too fast to stop. What's it going to be, hit the elderly couple, or hit the mom with her baby? Or are you going to build in a randomizer, leaving it up to chance, to soothe your conscience? In reality, you probably won't have to make that choice, since somebody else will have done that already for you. But what if you don't like their choice?

Let's say you are asked to program the self-driving car's response to a situation in which a choice needs to be made between hitting a pedestrian or crashing into a wall. Somebody in the higher echelons of your company has decided that the safest choice for the driver of the car is to hit the pedestrian – after all, the car company's concern is with the person who paid good money for the car, including its protective measures. Some would agree with such a train of thought, others would disagree. What if you disagree? Would you refuse to program this algorithm? Would you protest? What if you're the coach of this team that is asked to program it, and you disagree? Are you going to put your job on the line for your moral misgivings? Hard questions indeed.

The more intelligent the tech around us becomes, to more we will face moral questions. As I try to stress throughout the book, *awareness* is key. If you are aware of the moral dilemmas that are creeping up on us, and if you are aware of your own and other people's biases, prejudice, and stereotypes, that will help in making moral decisions, not just for yourself, but also for the organization you work at.

Empathy

If there is one word that has stormed the hit parades, then it's "empathy". Google has a tool named the *Google Books Ngram Viewer*, which shows the usage of a word or a phrase over time. If you look up the word "empathy", you can see the line in the graph near zero until the 1920s. Then it slowly rises gradually until around 1990. Then the graph shoots up steeply. Only in the last few years the increase of its usage seems to slow down a tiny bit. But still, the word *empathy* has grown in popularity enormously in the last few decades. Scroll through your social media time lines and see it popping up left and right. Many coaches and coaching tracks put a lot of stress on having *empathy* –

vicariously experiencing the feelings and thoughts of someone else. Leadership coaches enjoin the leaders of today's organizations to show true leadership by employing empathy – with employees, with other leaders, with stakeholders, and with the surroundings of the organization. Leadership that callously ignores the pleas of others and merely aims to please its own and its stakeholders' coffers is considered outdated and simply not done anymore – morally abject. Feeling the pain of others, being able to see the world through someone else's eyes, and taking the feelings and thoughts of others into account when making decisions is considered to be part of modern leadership. Even though this rings undeniably true to most, probably, there is a caveat to be made. Empathy is not always the best counselor when it comes to leadership and decision making.

Against Empathy

We've already encountered Paul Bloom in the previous segment about *morality*, and Bloom has more to say about *empathy* as well. In his thought-provoking 2016 book *Against Empathy*, he unfolds the downsides of empathy. For one, it's more difficult to feel empathy for a large group than it is to feel empathy for one individual. Charity organizations have known this for decades already. If you receive a request to donate to a charity, they almost always show you pictures and share stories about one individual in need. One child that looks miserable and needs to be fed, or one dog with the saddest eyes possible that looks straight into the camera to pull on your heartstrings. They know you'll be much more inclined to donate if you feel empathic than if you don't, and that empathy is best invoked by making things small, close, and personal. That effect on your empathic feelings is usually a good thing. You'll feel a whole lot more empathy for your own child than you do for a child halfway around the world that you've never seen, and that is good – I think we can all agree. But if you compare that same effect to a situation at work, things get messy. I've seen it happen. Some employee who's pretty good at chatting and fostering relations, hooks up with a higher manager in a hallway. They chat and laugh, and the employee makes a case for something they would love to have at the office. Think of a certain type of coffee machine, a foosball table, a vending machine, you name it, something that this particular employee likes very much, but not all employees per se. Others prefer different options. It could very well be the case that what this chatty employee wants, is wanted by only a small minority, but the higher manager now feels heaps of empathy for this employee because of their newfound connection and will in return do their utmost to fulfill the wishes of this one employee. You can imagine the looks on the faces and the thoughts in the minds of the other employees. This example involves only an innocent extra on the work floor, but this might as well be over something more profound, the empathic effect works the same and is by far from fair.

If you think of the biases, prejudice, stereotypes, and moreover, the in-groups and out-groups we discussed in earlier chapters, then it should be clear that we might feel more empathy for one group or individual over another for all the wrong reasons. Let me make this more clear with an extreme example. Right-wing white supremacists feel a lot of empathy for other white people who share their ideas, which makes them act real nice to those who are part of their little in-group. At the same time, these people feel no remorse treating non-white people horrendously, to the point of committing murder. If you take an honest look at history, you will find plenty of examples of empathy for one group leading to the eventual massacre of another group. Feeling empathy for your in-group causes you to dehumanize and objectify out-groups. If a member of an out-group hurts a member of your in-group, your intense feelings of empathy for the victim might very well make you do horrible thing to the perpetrator of the out-group.

On a less extreme scale we can see this downside of empathy at play in other ways than the beforementioned example of the chatty employee. If the boardroom of the company is filled with old, grey-haired white men, they will naturally feel more empathy for other white men – they won't even need to do that on purpose, we humans are wired to feel more empathy for people who are in our in-groups. Perhaps I should rephrase that, it's not only humans who feel that way. English primatologist and anthropologist Jane Goodall (1934) noticed during her many years of researching chimpanzee behavior that the apes are truly empathic towards the members of their own community, but as soon as they find a member of another community trespassing their borders, the first and foremost instinct is to attack and kill the poor soul.

Let me emphasize that not all about empathy is bad. On the contrary, being able to instinctively feel what others feel will help you a lot in life. People with a total lack of empathy – like narcissists, psychopaths, and sociopaths – are not exactly "pearls of society". Considering, however, the possible negative influence of empathy on leadership and decision making, we need to figure out how to overcome this downside of empathy. Bloom hands us a possible solution in the form of what he calls *rational compassion*. Bloom and other psychologists make a distinction between empathy and compassion by describing empathy as *feeling* exactly what someone else is feeling, and compassion as *understanding* exactly what someone else is feeling. Bloom maintains in his book that we have the capacity to circumvent feeling *too* much what others feel – thus impeding on our own judgment – and proposes instead to make more use of *rational compassion*. This would mean applying *system two* thinking – slow thinking – and using the awareness of, and knowledge about biases to make better founded decisions.

Back to the boardroom. A more diverse boardroom will naturally be more empathic to a lot more people than just to white men, thus leading to more diverse hiring and promoting. In some organizations we already see such a shift taking place, and the future will likely bring more and more of these changes for the better.

WEIRD and Beyond

A lot of psychological research of the past has been conducted on American white male psychology students, or rather, on WEIRD people. WEIRD is an acronym which stands for *Western, Educated, and from Industrialized, Rich, and Democratic countries*. In practice, much psychological research has been carried out with undergraduates from top universities in the United States. In 2010, researchers from the University of British Columbia published the results of a study that concluded that 68 percent of research subjects hailed from the United States, and a whopping 96 percent came from Western nations. Of the American subjects, 67 percent were undergraduates studying psychology.

Of course the availability played a big role in this habit to hire WEIRD. It's easy to conduct research on a group of people that is right there on campus, big enough, and readily available at low cost or no costs at all for the researchers. The problem is that psychologists have made a lot of assumptions about the general application of their findings. Results found in smalls groups of people were easily extrapolated to be true for humankind in general. In recent years – and this will continue into the foreseeable future – many experiments of the past were replicated to include much more diverse experimental and control groups. Some past results and conclusions have been taken into doubt because of these more diverse replications.

Take for instance the famous *Stanford Prison Experiment*, conducted by American psychologist Philip Zimbardo (1933) in 1971. In the experiment, an advertisement was placed to get students of Stanford to participate in a study on prison behavior of both prisoners and guards. For each student that volunteered, a coin was flipped to see if they became a prisoner or a guard. The basement of Stanford University was used to mock a prison environment. As it turned out, the "guards" became so enthralled by their role that they went overboard with their performances and caused real harm – mostly psychological – to the "prisoners". Several "prisoners" quit after only a few days into the experiment and the whole thing was blown off after only six days. Zimbardo and his experiment gained eternal fame and the results have been used over and over again to rail against prison abuse and authoritarian systems. Over the years, however, several issues with the famous experiment arose, and certainly one of them was the fact that all participants were predominantly white male middle class students. The outcome of the experiment could have been a lot different if the group of participants had been more diverse, and indeed, later replications have shown different outcomes, not by far as radical as the original experiment.

Studies into cultural differences in relation to social psychology have shown that different cultural values result in different test results, also on the individual level. For instance, in many Asian cultures, there is much emphasis on strength in groups and less on the individual, whereas in Western cultures that is exactly the other way around, with American culture being the pinnacle of individualization.

As you can see, the future of psychology is still in motion, there's still so much to (re-)explore. With our modern organizations moving even more in the direction of collective knowledge hubs which thrive on human interaction, I can only foresee more use for and value of knowledge about psychology.

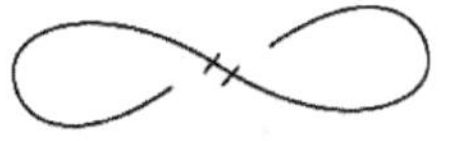

Chapter Six – The History of Psychology

Since you're still reading this I assume you've decided to go for the in-depth look at where today's psychological insights originate from, good! Let's first see how science actually defines psychology. According to Gray and Bjorklund's eighth edition of the comprehensive and widely used introductory psychology textbook – aptly named "Psychology" – the definition is as follows.

A definition of psychology

Psychology is the science of behavior and the mind. *Behavior* refers to the observable actions of an individual, either human or animal, and *mind* refers to an individual's sensations, perceptions, memories, thoughts, dreams, motives, emotions, and other subjective experiences.

According to Gray and Bjorklund, it also refers to all of the unconscious knowledge and operating rules that are built into or stored in the brain, and that provides the foundation for organizing behavior and conscious experience.

Science refers to all attempts to answer questions through the systematic collection and logical analysis of objectively observable data. Gray and Bjorklund add that most of the data in psychology are based on observations of behavior because behavior is directly observable and mind is not. Be that as it may, psychologists often use those data to make inferences about the mind.

The first modern psychologist

If we look back into history, psychology as such is not yet that old. It wasn't until 1879 that Wilhelm Wundt (1832-1920) opened the first official psychology laboratory in Leipzig, Germany. So as a modern science, it's not even one and a half-century old. In earlier eras, however, psychology-related topics were raised mostly by philosophers. Thus, psychology can be traced back as far as thousands of years, for instance to the world of the Ancient Greeks – with Socrates, Plato, and Aristotle – and in the Far East to the times of Confucius and Buddha.

If we take a closer look at Western philosophy in more recent centuries, we find the basics of psychology as we know it today.

Matter over mind

In seventeenth-century France, René Descartes (1596-1650) proclaimed the now-famous sentence, *"Cogito ergo sum"*, "I think, therefore I am". Until Descartes, the understanding of who and what we are was mainly subject to religious views. The Cartesian *dualistic* view maintained that we humans consist of a material body and an immaterial soul. Most of our inner workings were attributed to the soul. Descartes, however, submitted that most of what we do, such as eating, drinking, sleeping, walking, et cetera, could just as well be purely mechanical. Only thinking, Descartes implied, was different. That, he attributed to the soul.

Descartes did put a lot of stress on the tight relationship between body and soul. He was quite aware, albeit in a rudimentary fashion, of the existence of a nervous system. Descartes' view was that the soul interacted with the body from a part of the brain, through these "threads", with the parts of the body.

Meanwhile, in England, there was a certain Thomas Hobbes (1588-1679), who took things in quite a different direction. He argued that we have no soul at all and that all there is, is matter and energy. This is a view known as *materialism*. In Hobbes' view, all thought is the result of purely mechanical processes, mainly taking place in the brain. Thus, all of our behavior is subject to natural laws and can be asserted as such. This approach made it possible for a new view to enter the scene, *empiricism*.

Empiric agility

Here we already see the first connection with our modern business environments. No doubt have you heard of working in a so-called *Agile* environment. Maybe you've even heard a coach or consultant say that "the *Scrum* framework is based on *empiricism*". For those of you not already familiar with these terms, I will go into more detail in the next chapter, but for now, a short explanation will have to suffice. Scrum is a framework for developing complex products, such as software programs. Scrum falls under the *Agile* umbrella of methods used to deliver valuable products as early as possible to the customer and continuously after that. While traditional *project management* is mostly based on estimated planning ahead, *Agile* methodologies – like *Scrum* – look back on what has recently been accomplished, to try and forecast the near future.

Empiricism in psychology refers to the idea that knowledge and thought derive from *sensory* experiences, like vision, smell, touch, et cetera. Our senses provide the input that allows us to think about the world and behave adaptively within it. Similarly, the *Scrum Guide* states that "empiricism asserts that knowledge comes from experience and [entails] making decisions based on what is known."

As always, every theory or movement is followed by a counter-theory or movement. The opposite of empiricism is *nativism*, which states that the most basic forms of human knowledge and the basic operating characteristics of the mind are native to the human mind – they are inborn and need not be acquired through experience.

While *empiricist* philosophy flourished in England, *nativist* philosophy took root in Germany. The most famous of nativist thinkers is no doubt Immanuel Kant (1724-1804). He distinguished between *a priori* knowledge, built into the brain, and *a posteriori* knowledge, which is gained from experience.

The Theory of Evolution

Now we stumble upon arguably the most fundamental of all ideas ever conceived by any human. Where Kant had an idea of innate knowledge, he had no explanation for it or it's workings. Then Charles Darwin (1809-1882) came along.

Darwin's idea was that all living creatures evolve over time. Random mutations in genetic material take place all the time. Through natural selection, Darwin argued, a specimen of a species that, through these random mutations, is the best fit for their environment will live longer and produce the most offspring. As a result, the hereditary genetic material with the best-fit qualities will prevail over the less-fit genetic material.

From Darwin onwards, it was conceivable how natural selection could have formed inborn knowledge in living beings that would have provided them with an advantage over those without that innate knowledge

Back to Wilhelm Wundt in 1879. Wundt and his students worked very hard to get psychology on the scientific map, separate from philosophy and biology. Within a decade, psychology laboratories opened up all around the globe and psychological experiments were carried out in multitudes and with rigor. It was important for these early psychologists to be seen as proper scientists who did a serious and worthy job with their experimental psychology. In the end, that worked out properly. A survey published in *American Psychologist* in 1991 ranked Wundt's reputation as first for "all-time eminence" based on ratings provided by 29 American historians of psychology. But before the praise, *Freud* happened.

Freud

It will be hard to find anyone who will not name Sigmund Freud first when asked to name a famous psychologist. Popular as his name is today, so was he during his lifetime. His influence on twentieth-century thinking is only rivaled by Charles Darwin or Karl Marx. And this much to the chagrin of experimental psychologists like Wundt and his followers. Unlike the meticulous scientific approach of earlier psychologists, Freud (1856-1939), and famous disciples like Carl-Gustav Jung (1875-1961), wielded a very different instrument to pry the mind.

Freud was the inventor of *psychoanalysis*, a form of *psychodynamic psychotherapy*. Basically, he talked to his "patients" and encouraged them to talk about their dreams and to engage in *free association*, which entails sharing thoughts freely without reservation and much concentration, basically blurting out whatever comes to mind when confronted with a word given by the therapist. The goal of *psychoanalysis* was to bring *unconscious*, or what Freud called *repressed*, thoughts and feelings to the forefront so that the patient is relieved from suffering from harmful emotions.

Over the years, Freud developed numerous theories. Many of us are familiar with his focus on the meaning of dreams, sexually repressed memories, the Oedipus complex, penis-envy, et cetera. Perhaps you've even heard of the *Id*, the *Ego* and the *Super-ego*, with which Freud described, in 1923 – in his work "The Ego and the Id" – the instinctual desires (the *Id*), the morals (the *Super-ego*), and the mediating self (the *Ego*). Freud hoped that his theories about the unconscious mind and his subsequent research would provide a solid scientific foundation for his therapeutic technique.

Many of Freud's theories have since been debunked as *pseudoscience*. Even in his days, Wilhelm Wundt remained skeptical about all hypotheses that operated with the concept of "the unconscious". The famous science philosopher Karl Popper (1902-1994), who argued that all proper scientific theories must be potentially *falsifiable*, claimed that Freud's psychoanalytic theories were presented in *unfalsifiable* form, meaning that no experiment could ever disprove them. To give you an example of what Popper meant, consider the following dialogue between therapist and patient.

"I see," proclaimed the therapist, "all you've said today points to the fact that you hate your mother."

Heavily shaking his head, the patient replies, "Not at all! I love my mother dearest!"

"Ah," all but whispered the therapist, "or so you think! Unconsciously, however, you hate her guts!"

Today, many therapists believe strongly in the unconscious and the impact of early childhood experiences on the rest of a person's life. Psychodynamic psychotherapy, and its intensive form psychoanalysis, are widely used throughout the world as a form of therapy that is considered to be sufficiently proven effective by many. Patients are now called *clients* and the client is not necessarily lying down on a couch while trying to gain insight into their unconscious hindrances. Typically, clients have several one-hour sessions per week with their therapist, for as long as twenty weeks or more in a row. The bond that is formed between client and therapist is considered to be of great importance to the final result of the therapy.

As Isaac Newton proposed, every action has an opposite and equal reaction. After the first peak of the popularity of Freud and his focus on the unconscious, a very different movement got hold of especially the United States, England, and Russia, namely, *behaviorism*.

Behaviorism

You've probably heard of one of the most famous behaviorists, the Russian physiologist Ivan Pavlov (1849-1936), or rather, his dog. Well, to be fair, not actually *his* dog, but the dogs he and his colleagues did tests with in their laboratory. Initially, Pavlov and his colleagues wanted to investigate the differences in salivation when dogs were given different kinds of food. Much to the frustration of Pavlov's colleagues, however, whenever the dogs realized food was coming soon, by hearing a buzzer sound, they already started to salivate, without even having food in their mouths. Pavlov found this so interesting that he posed a new thesis and started the now famous behaviorist experiments.

In the experiments conducted by Pavlov, he demonstrated what is now known as *classical conditioning*. It is important to understand this form of conditioning since it is referred to and used frequently in the business world.

- In *classical conditioning*, we start with a neutral stimulus, like the buzzer sounding, which has a neutral response (no response). And we start with an unconditioned stimulus, the food, and an unconditioned response, salivation.
- In stage two, the neutral stimulus (the buzzer) is linked to the unconditioned stimulus (the food), which produces the unconditioned response (the salivation).
- In the third and final stage, the buzzer has become the conditioned stimulus that triggers the now conditioned response of salivation.

The food is no longer in the equation, but the effect won't last forever, it will degrade over time and use. If the buzzer keeps sounding without food appearing, the salivation will cease to be triggered.

In the world of psychology, however, Pavlov is not the most famous behaviorist. A certain B.F. Skinner takes that prize, along with John B. Watson, both American psychologists. Watson (1878-1958) established *behaviorism* through his address "Psychology as the Behaviorist Views It", which was given at Columbia University in 1913. He became particularly famous, or rather, from a current point of view, *notorious*, for conducting classical conditioning experiments on an 11-month-old boy affectionately named "Little Albert", in 1920. Watson and his colleague Rosalie Rayner presented Little Albert with a rat, which he found to be a nice playmate at first. But after a few times of displaying the rat, quickly followed by a loud bang of a hammer on a steel bar, poor Little Albert became absolutely frightened of the rat. He even became fearful of other small furry animals, like rabbits. These days, *unethical* experiments like this could never be repeated. No one in their right mind would want to put a child – or even an adult – through such a traumatizing experience, and no one would be allowed to by ethics committees that are now in place at universities and other lab environments everywhere.

B.F. Skinner became probably the most famous of the behaviorists with his *Skinner boxes*. Because of his particular last name, this sounds worse than it actually is. Skinner (1904-1990) got his idea for his boxes from Edward Thorndike (1874-1949), who designed puzzle boxes for cats. A cat was placed inside a box with a door that could be opened by the cat by stepping on a lever. That way, the cat could reach the food outside the box. The difference with Pavlov's dogs was that Thorndike's cats actually had some control over their environment, they were "operators" in their boxes, operating levers. Hence the name of this type of conditioning, *operant conditioning*. In 1898, Thorndike advanced his "Law of Effect", which states that responses that produce a satisfying effect in a particular situation become more likely to occur again in that situation, and responses that produce a discomforting effect become less likely to occur again in that situation.

Skinner believed that learning new things could be achieved without too much mental work. Simply trying things and finding out what is effective, would do the trick. His *Skinner boxes* were slightly different from Thorndike's boxes for cats. Skinners boxes had levers and handles and other operable options for the animals inside, but the animals stayed inside the box throughout the session. Instead, they did receive rewards, like small pieces of food, but still inside the box. What Skinner found was that at the first trial, animals would try anything to get out, like scratch, dig, push, claw, howl, push levers, etc. When something resulted in a piece of food, like pushing a lever, the animals would, after a few trials, stop doing the other things and just push the lever to get some food.

If you'd happen to walk into his laboratory when performing a later trial, it would seem amazing that the animal apparently knows exactly how to get the food. *Operant conditioning* has its way of getting results. This did not go unnoticed. Especially further research that Skinner did on what he called *partial reinforcement*, was of great interest to, for instance, the gambling industry. As it turns out, you don't have to reward an animal – or human – every single time they perform a certain operation. If you reward them intermittently, say, every other time (*fixed-ratio* schedule), or after a random number of times (*variable-ratio* schedule), it still works. In other words, even if you only win every now and then at a slot machine, you still keep throwing in the coins. The reverse is also true, by the way. If you have a whining kid and you keep saying, "no, you can't get ice cream!", but at the umpteenth whine, you cave in, then all you've taught your kid is to keep whining because now they know that – eventually – they will get their reward.

The trouble with behaviorism is that every piece of the behavior of an individual can be explained away by deducting and reducing every action to a result of a previous stimulus. Thus, learning new things can be explained without reference to the mind or consciousness, which in turn reduces not being able to learn to laziness. You just need to put in the necessary hours of work to reach higher levels, is the basic idea.

In this light, a popular myth that keeps popping up every now and then is the "10,000 hours rule". Malcolm Gladwell (1963) stated in his book "Outliers" (2008) that 10,000 hours of *deliberate practice* in a certain field makes you an expert in it. Even though Gladwell himself said later on that his idea about the 10,000 hours was often misunderstood (2014), the typical behaviorist notion can still be encountered in both business and sports. Gladwell added that "natural ability requires a huge investment of time in order to be made manifest". But a Princeton study tears that theory down. In a meta-analysis of 88 studies on deliberate practice, the researchers found that practice accounted for a mere 12% difference in performance in various domains.

Self-actualization

Of course – yet again – there was a counter-movement to this and the previous stream within psychology. Some psychologists didn't like the idea that everything we do is determined by the unconscious. Neither did they like the idea of behaviorism's simplifications. Instead, people like Abraham Maslow (1908-1970) and Carl Rogers (1902-1987) began to form their own ideas about personal control, intentionality, and a human predisposition for "good" as important for our self-concept and our behavior.

Maslow first coined his now well-known concept of a *hierarchy of needs* in the form of a pyramid in 1943. At the bottom of the pyramid, we find the most basic of human needs, which are basic *physical* needs, like breathing, drinking, eating, sleeping, sex, etc. We go up one level to *safety*, which also includes, for instance, morality and health. In the middle, we find *love and belonging*, like family, friendship, and intimacy. At the fourth level, the so-called *cognitive* level, we see esteem, like self-esteem, achievement, confidence, but also respect from others. At the top, the *aesthetic* level, we find what Maslow called *self-actualization*, which evolves around creativity, problem-solving, lack of prejudice, but also, acceptance of facts. Even though the pyramid suggests that one can only fulfill their needs one level at a time, Maslow in later life concluded that self-actualization was not an automatic outcome of satisfying the lower levels.

What baffled me at first, is that Maslow proposed his idea of the hierarchy of needs in the midst of a world war. I wondered if anyone in those dreadful times rose above the lower levels of the pyramid. But apparently, the horrors of war inspired a vision of peace in Maslow, leading to his groundbreaking psychological studies of self-actualizing.

Carl Rogers is widely considered to be one of the founders of *psychotherapy research*, with his unique person-centered approach. This *humanistic* angle provided "unconditional positive regard, accepting a person without negative judgment of a person's basic worth".

These *humanists* had a great influence on our workplaces throughout the second half of the twentieth century and beyond.

The cognitive revolution

Albert Bandura (1925) – now known as the greatest living psychologist – provided a much-needed bridge from the behaviorists towards *cognitive psychology* with his *social-cognitive theory*. Bandura noticed that you can learn new things not just by experiencing conditioning yourself, but also by observing someone else undergoing conditioning. This is described by psychologists as *observational learning*.

Another influential figure in the *cognitive revolution* was Noam Chomsky (1928), also still alive today. Chomsky is foremost a linguist. He rejected the *radical behaviorist* theory of Skinner, who posed that all we learn is a result of our interactions with others and our environments. Informed by what Chomsky knew about language, he challenged the idea of the *tabula rasa*, or blank slate theory – the idea that we all start with nothing. Based on observations of language acquisition and the rich linguistic competence which children obtain, Chomsky maintained that syntactic knowledge is at least partially innate to humans. As an example of linguistic competence, you can think of our ability to form an infinite number of sentences, including ones we've never heard before. Even sentences that never before have been uttered in our language.

The cognitive psychologists strived to apply *the scientific method* to the study of human knowledge, which meant maintaining a healthy skepticism about human observations, given that assumptions or biases will distort how one interprets their own observations. Therefore, as part of the cognitive revolution, during the last few decades of the twentieth century, stretching to the current, we've seen a growing influence of *computer science*, and all that comes with it, in the world of psychology. *Neuroscience* is to this day a hot topic and still hasn't piqued interest. What is clear, however, is that psychologists have cemented the *cognitive revolution*, as people realized that *cognition* was crucial to the understanding of human behavior.

Psychology these days

Nowadays, psychology is practiced by many people, with very different backgrounds and interests. From therapists to business coaches, from neuroscientists to community workers, from economists to police officers, all of them use at least bits and pieces of psychological knowledge.

Psychologies' basic types are now commonly named Abnormal, Biological, Cognitive, Developmental, Experimental, Evolutionary, Mathematical, Neuro, Personality, Psychophysics, and Social psychology. It would be too much to dive into each and every one of these forms of psychology here in this work, but it gives you some idea of the diversity and depth of psychology today.

Now that we've seen the beginning and the growth of modern psychology, it is time to explore the almost analogous evolution of modern work…

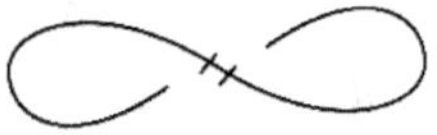

Chapter Seven – The History of Work

People have been working since the dawn of our time. Whether it was hunting or gathering, farming or nursing, warring, or leading, work has always been there. But, work has changed over time. With the discovery of fire, the creation of tools, and the ever-increasing complexities of our human societies, labor has evolved for most humans.

Understanding the Why

If we would focus solely on today's modern workplace – the one you are probably familiar with – we would be missing out on *why* things came to be as they currently are. To better understand the current, it definitely helps to understand the past. Thus, a brief dive into history, similar to the previous chapter about psychology, will aid in comprehending the earlier chapters that dealt with psychological insights into the way things happen in your work environment today.

Let me be frank about the scope of this all too brief overview of the history of work. No doubt I will be skipping numerous significant influential persons as well as events, but by no means is this chapter – nor the previous one – intended as an all-encompassing encyclopedia of sorts. I will touch on topics that I see as highly influential still to this day, and therefore important to understand.

East India Companies

Every era has had its radical changes in labor. Imagine the time when the wheel was invented and the effect it had on what could be done in a day's work. Imagine the invention of boats and what it brought and changed in our lives. Let's skip a few millennia and imagine the huge ocean faring ships that went from Europe to Asia and brought back spices and other valuable merchandise – which resulted in enormous European wealth.

We start our story here – around the year 1600 – because the *Dutch East India Company* and the *British East India Company* were the world's first *multinational corporations*. They pioneered features that later became textbook characteristics of *modern corporations* – a permanent capital, legal personhood, separation of ownership and management, limited liability for shareholders and for directors, and tradable shares.

From a psychological perspective, this is important. It meant that the managers were not the owners of the company and vice versa – which gave the managers a sense of freedom to take risks that the owners might not have taken in their position. The limited liability, which meant shareholders were legally responsible for the debts of a company only to the extent of the nominal value of their shares, resulted in even more psychological freedom for managers to do as they saw fit.

These two companies – arguably the largest companies the world has ever seen, and that includes today's giants like Apple, Google, and Microsoft – reigned the globe for more than two centuries and amassed such power and wealth that they were almost states in their own right, providing jobs for many millions around the world.

Cardwell's Law – after the British historian Donald Cardwell (1919-1998) – states that every society, when left on its own, will be technologically creative for only short periods. In a way, *Cardwell's Law* is applicable to businesses as well. Cardwell examined the history of nations and saw that the rise and fall of societies and their technological advances and accompanying successes were only shortlived. Sooner or later conservative forces took over and grinded to a halt the progress that had made the society so successful. This is what happened with the East India Companies as well. After two centuries, the agility of the companies was totally gone, which led to both their downfalls.

Translated to today's businesses, we actually see the same. Most companies are successful with a certain product or service for a relatively short time, before conservative forces assert their influence by managing everything to death. Any new initiatives – be it technological or organizational – are deemed too risky and are therefore managed out of the way through the institutional channels available in large organizations. How many of you recognize *the powers that be* at work in your organization?

As a sidenote, Frenchman René Descartes – mentioned in the previous chapter and one of the founders of modern philosophy – lived in the Dutch Republic for about 20 years (1629-1649), which at that time prospered because of the wealth and power of the Dutch East India Company.

Industrial Revolutions

From the dusk of the *East India Companies*, we see the dawn of the *First Industrial Revolution*, which started around 1760 in Britain. During this period, there was a huge transition from manual to machine production methods, aided by the use of steam and water power. This changed almost every aspect of the way people worked and lived in those days.

The *Second Industrial Revolution*, also known as the *Technical Revolution*, started around 1870. While the First Revolution heralded concepts like *interchangeable parts* and *mass production*, the Second Revolution was characterized by the increased production of *railroads*, large-scale iron and steel production, the widespread use of machinery in manufacturing, increased use of steam power, the widespread use of the *telegraph*, use of petroleum and the beginning of *electrification*. It was also the period during which *modern organizational methods for operating large scale businesses* came into use.

Railroads are credited by scholars such as Alfred D. Chandler (1918-2007), with creating *the modern business enterprise*. A railroad required expertise available across the whole length of its trackage to deal with daily crises, breakdowns, and bad weather. A collision in Massachusetts (US) in 1841 led to a call for safety reform. This led to the reorganization of railroads into different departments with clear lines of management authority. When the telegraph became available, companies built telegraph lines along the railroads to keep track of trains. Does anyone recognize the term "line management" here?

To indulge your historical awareness, it might be of interest to note that it was in 1912 that Henry Gantt invented his famous, or – depending on your perspective – notorious, Gantt Chart. Gantt (1861-1919) had a less famous predecessor in Karol Adamiecki (1866-1933), who developed his similar Harmonogram much earlier, in 1896, but did so in Polish and Russian, thereby missing out on eternal fame in the English-speaking world.

Scientific management

During the *Second Industrial Revolution*, Frederick Winslow Taylor (1856-1915) and others in America developed the concept of "scientific management", or *Taylorism*. At almost the same time in France, Henri Fayol (1841-1925), a mining engineer, developed his general theory of business administration, known as *Fayolism*.

Scientific management initially concentrated on reducing the steps taken in performing work, such as bricklaying or shoveling, by using analysis such as *time-and-motion* studies, but the concepts evolved into fields such as industrial engineering, manufacturing engineering, and business management that helped to completely restructure the operations of factories.

Taylor's core principles included replacing rule-of-thumb work methods with methods based on a scientific study of the tasks, scientifically selecting, training, and developing each employee rather than passively leaving them to train themselves, providing "detailed instruction and supervision of each worker in the performance of that worker's discrete task", dividing work nearly equally between managers and workers, such that the managers apply *scientific management* principles to planning the work and the workers actually performing the tasks.

A contemporary of Taylor was Max Weber (1864-1920), often referred to as one of the founders of *sociology*. Weber embraced the view that *direct hierarchy* was the best form of leadership for larger organizations. Weber's *bureaucratic* theory or model is sometimes also known as the "rational-legal" model. The model tries to explain bureaucracy from a rational point of view.

Weber wrote that the modern bureaucracy in both the public and private sector relies on the general principle of precisely defined and organized competencies of the various offices. These competencies are underpinned by rules, laws, or administrative regulations. For Weber, this meant:

- A rigid division of labor is established that clearly identifies regular tasks and duties of the particular bureaucratic system.
- Regulations describe firmly established chains of command and the duties and capacity to coerce others to comply.
- Hiring people with particular, certified qualifications supports regular and continuous execution of the assigned duties.

Weber noted that these three aspects constitute the essence of *bureaucratic management*. Characteristic attributes encountered in a bureaucratically managed organization are, according to Weber:

- Specialized roles.
- Recruitment based on merit (e.g., tested through open competition).
- Uniform principles of placement, promotion, and transfer in an administrative system.
- Careerism with systematic salary structure.
- Hierarchy, responsibility, and accountability.
- The subjection of official conduct to strict rules of discipline and control.
- The supremacy of abstract rules.
- Impersonal authority.
- Political neutrality.

To those with a certain affection for the aforementioned *Agile* way of working, the works of Taylor and Weber will send shivers down the spine. They had however also contemporaries who thought in very different ways. Take for instance Mary Parker Follett (1868-1933), an American social worker who, eventually, became known as the "Mother of Modern Management". Instead of emphasizing industrial and mechanical components, Follett advocated for what she saw as the far more important *human element*, regarding people as the most valuable within any business. She was one of the first theorists to actively write about the role people had on effective management, and discuss the importance of learning to deal with and promote positive human relations as a fundamental aspect.

Follett's work came during the height of Frederick Taylor's *Scientific management* movement, which advocated the "one right way" for tasks to be performed, and Weber's lauding of bureaucracy. Follett's 1926 essay "The Giving of Orders" challenged both Taylor's and Weber's suppositions and presented an alternative to purely top-down hierarchy in management.

Follett defined management as "the art of getting things done through people". In her essay, she addressed issues of authority in business management. She found that people respond better to situations than to top-down orders and managers should give people the means and willingness to respond to given situations instead of merely giving orders: "My solution is to depersonalize the giving of orders, to unite all concerned in a study of the situation, to discover the law of the situation, and obey that." To those with an *Agile* mindset, this sounds a lot better than the stern ideas of Taylor and Weber.

Follett did for a brief period during her lifetime have a huge influence. For instance, her pioneering understanding of lateral processes within hierarchical organizations led directly to the formation of *matrix-style organizations*, the first of which was DuPont, in the 1920s.

Unfortunately, many of her ideas were largely cast aside for decades, for cringe-worthy reasons. One is the purely sexist reason that Follett was a woman in an age when men still ruled absolute. The other being the perception that her ideas were too far ahead of her time. And so befalls the fate of the prescient.

Another pioneering woman was Lillian Moller Gilbreth (1878-1972), an American psychologist and industrial engineer who applied psychology to the workplace. She is considered to be the first *industrial/organizational psychologist*. Gilbreth and her husband were very adept at performing *time-and-motion* studies. This *business efficiency* technique became a major part of *scientific management*. What it basically comes down to, is measuring the amount of time a certain motion takes and see where and how that time can be improved. While studying for her Ph.D. at the University of California, Gilbreth's dissertation was published in 1914 as "The Psychology of Management: The Function of the Mind in Determining, Teaching and Installing Methods of Least Waste". Many of you will recognize the terminology later found in so-called *Lean Management* techniques, which focus heavily on eliminating waste in processes.

In today's business environments, a desire for measuring worker output, or perhaps team output, is commonplace. Often, this measurement wish is linked to a perceived need for both an elimination of waste and an increase in the output. The following tale from the early twentieth-century warrants some restraint in this area.

From 1924 until 1932, experiments were done at the *Hawthorne Works*, just outside Chicago. At Hawthorne, workers, many of them women, made telephone relays, amongst other electrical items. Over the course of several years, different teams of women were tested in specific experiment rooms, within which conditions were adjusted to see what effect that would have on the measured output of the women. The most famous of adjustments was that of the light intensity. But there were many other changes made to see in what way they affected productivity, like having clean work stations or not, clearing floors of obstacles or not, the amount of ventilation, the amount and length of breaks, start and end times of the workday, et cetera. The invariable results of any of these changes were that the productivity went up, even when the conditions were reset to those of the starting phase, much to the surprise of the researchers.

In 1958, Henry A. Landsberger, in his work "Hawthorne Revisited", concluded that the productivity gain occurred as a result of the motivational effect on the workers, caused merely by the interest being shown in them. This he coined the *Hawthorne Effect*. Later this effect also became known as the *observer-expectancy effect*, which stipulates that a researcher's *cognitive bias* causes them to subconsciously influence the participants of an experiment. We'll return to cognitive bias and many more biases in later chapters.

After World War II, we saw an enormous investment in the economies worldwide. In Germany and Austria, for instance, we behold *Das Wirtschaftswunder* when these countries rise above the rubble of the war and dash to the forefront of prosperity in the world. Other European countries prosper as well, especially with the help of the American economic Marshall Plan, which was put into effect to counter the surge of Communism and to provide for a stable economic partnership.

Project Management

In 1954 we see a few interesting facts arise. In that year, US Air Force General Bernard Schriever (1910-2005) coined the term "project management" and Peter Drucker (1909-2005) wrote *The Practice of Management* in which he describes his idea of *Management by objectives*. These facts are interesting because they resonate to this day when it comes to the way organizations are run.

Project management is described as the practice of initiating, planning, executing, controlling, and closing the work of a team to achieve specific goals and meet specific success criteria at the specified time. In short, a project is successful if its scope is delivered within time, within budget, and with specified quality.

Management by objectives is the process of defining specific objectives within an organization that management can convey to organization members, then deciding how to achieve each objective in sequence. This process allows managers to consider the work that needs to be done one step at a time to allow for a calm, yet productive work environment. This process also helps organization members to see their accomplishments as they achieve each objective, which reinforces a positive work environment and a sense of achievement, according to Drucker.

Interestingly, the concept of *Management by objectives* draws on the ideas presented by Mary Parker Follett decades before. A stipulation of *Management by objectives* submits that when employees themselves have been involved with the goal-setting and choosing the course of action to be followed by them, they are more likely to fulfill their responsibilities.

According to fellow founder of *Management by objectives*, George Odiorne (1920-1992), the system can be described as a process whereby the superior and subordinate jointly identify common goals, define each individual's major areas of responsibility in terms of the results expected of him or her, and use these measures as guides for operating the work unit and assessing the contribution of each of its members. An important part of *Management by objectives* is the measurement and comparison of an employee's actual performance with the standards that were set.

Note that much of this, however far in idea from Taylor or Weber, is still unnerving to the modern *Agile-minded* reader. The very words, "superior" and "subordinate" sound almost laughable to the younger reader, I'm sure. It is interesting to note that Drucker coined the term "knowledge worker" as early as 1959. Sometimes these dwellings in history provide surprising links between the past and the present.

I want to posit here that the ideas of Drucker and Follett did not find fertile ground in each and every organization. There were still many organizations, large and small, both public and private, that clung to the teachings of Taylor and Weber like moths to a flame. I dare say that even today, well on our way into the twenty-first century, there are still people who wholeheartedly believe that strict hierarchy and strict separation between "thinkers" (managers) and "doers" (workers) is key to achieving success. If success in the organizations where such people work is defined by keeping projects within what is called the *Iron Triangle* of scope, time, and budget, then perhaps those people are not so wrong, in their context.

Change Management

With so many organizational changes taking place, a new field of work emerged during the nineteen-sixties, namely *change management*. Many *change management* models and processes were based on *grief* studies. As consultants saw a correlation between grieving from the loss of a loved one and grieving among employees in an organization due to loss of jobs and departments, many early change models focused on *emotions* as employees mourned job-related transitions.

In 1962, in his work on the *diffusion of innovations*, Everett Rogers (1931-2004) posited that change must be understood in the context of the *time, communication,* and its *impact* on *all affected participants.* Placing *people* at the core of change thinking was a fundamental contribution to developing the concept of *change management.* Rogers proposed the well-known descriptive *Adopter* groups of how people respond to change: *Innovators, Early Adopters, Early Majority, Late Majority,* and *Laggards.*

In 1970, Milton Friedman (1912-2006), an American economist and advisor to U.S. President Ronald Reagan and U.K. Prime Minister Margaret Thatcher, powerfully championed a new ideal of shareholder primacy in a New York Times Magazine article entitled "The Social Responsibility of Business is to Increase its Profits." The influential American Business Roundtable, in their own words an "Association of Chief Executive Officers Committed to Improving Public Policy", voiced Friedman's ideal with the words that have in recent years attracted much disdain from many a side, "the paramount duty of management and of boards of directors is to the corporation's stockholders."

To some of you, no doubt, IPMA and PMI are well-known abbreviations. In 1965, the IPMA, or *International Project Management Association,* was founded, and in 1969, the PMI, the *Project Management Institute* was launched. This goes to show that *project management* as a serious business itself has been around for over half a century. People are from this period onwards getting certified through these institutes to prove their knowledge and understanding of project management in their resumes.

In 1977, the first *project management* software emerged, which further helped to etch project management into the way of working in especially larger organizations around the world. Speaking of software, one of the most common agitations of *Agile-minded* spirits is the widespread use of the *Waterfall Method* in traditional project management. The basic premise proposes a step-by-step approach to completing one piece of software that can be used by an end-user, a client.

For instance, if a manager asks for software to be built that helps the financial department automate the billing process, some people will first gather precise information on what needs to be built. Then some other people will design the architecture of the software. In the next step, yet another group of people will actually build the software by typing away on their computers, only to hand their work over to the next batch of people who are going to test it. Once all steps are taken, the final phase is described as *maintenance*, in which the new piece of software will linger until the end of time. Or when interest in it runs out, whichever comes first.

It must be said that the poor soul first describing this whole process in 1970, Winston Walker Royce (1929-1995), did not intend for his description to be taken so literally, as a prescription of a one time flow down a waterfall. Rather, Royce, who did not even coin the term "Waterfall" himself, proposed an *iterative, incremental* approach, where every step linked back to the previous. If ever project managers had understood Royce better, a lot of misery over the decades could have been avoided.

Back to project management itself. "PRojects IN Controlled Environments", or PRINCE, is a structured project management method that emphasizes dividing projects into manageable and controllable *stages*. PRINCE2 is the second edition of the earlier PRINCE method which was initially developed in 1989 by a UK government support agency. PRINCE2 was released in 1996 as *a generic project management method* and is still a *de-facto standard for project management* in many countries worldwide.

While *management by objectives* and traditional *project management* put heavy emphasis on maximizing *output*, W. Edwards Deming (1900-1993) tried to steer leaders in the industries towards maximizing *quality*. Deming has mostly become famous for his consulting work after the Second World War, in Japan, credited by many to be one of the inspirations for what is known as the Japanese post-war economic miracle, much like *Das Wirtschaftswunder* in Germany and Austria.

Deming championed the work of Walter Shewhart (1891-1967), including his *statistical process control*, a method of quality control which employs statistical methods to monitor and control a process, and what Deming called the "Shewhart Cycle", more commonly known as the *Plan-Do-Check-Act* cycle. Later, Deming provided his own version with the *Plan-Do-Study-Act* cycle, which, in the feelings of Deming, gave more poise to what Shewhart actually meant. The observant *Agile-minded* reader has no doubt spotted the very modern-sounding cycle we see return nowadays in an *Agile framework* like *Scrum*. Planning, sprinting, reviewing, and then planning again, basically coincide with what we see in Shewhart's cycle.

In 1982, Deming wrote *Quality, Productivity, and Competitive Position*, in which he offers a *theory of management* based on his now-famous *14 Points for Management*. Most notably amongst the points are the stress on constant quality improvement and the changing role of the leadership, from managing by numbers towards leadership that provides an environment of safety, constant training, and broken down barriers between departments. In the eyes of Deming, people in research, design, sales, and production must work as a team in order to provide for the best product or service. I find it pretty devastating that today, almost forty years onwards, coaches like myself still find ourselves struggling to tear down completely separately working silos within organizations.

The relatively new field of *change management* underwent some important developments in the nineteen-nineties. In his 1993 book, "Managing at the Speed of Change", Daryl Conner coined the term *burning platform* based on the 1988 North Sea Piper Alpha oil rig fire, with which he meant, a major crisis that urges the change of behavior. You will hear this term, *burning platform*, being used many times over in organizations, even though not many will have thought through what they're actually implying. Many *change managers* since have concluded that the whole idea of the burning platform does not really work since, in itself, the notion brings about nothing but anxiety. And anxiety is not a very good catalyst for lasting change.

Perhaps the most notable name in the whole of change management is John P. Kotter (1947). In 1996, his book *Leading Change* was published. In the preface, Kotter says the original articles, which preceded the book and were printed in the *Harvard Business Review* in 1995, unexpectedly struck a chord with managers, many of whom recognized in Kotter's texts real-life examples of what they experienced first-hand went wrong in their organizations when undertaking the so-manieth organizational change. A second reason for the book's success is attributed to the enclosed eight-phase plan for change, which serves as a blueprint and helps people to discuss transformation, problems, and strategies for change.

These are Kotter's eight steps:

1. Create a Sense of Urgency
2. Build a Guiding Coalition
3. Form a Strategic Vision and Initiatives
4. Enlist a Volunteer Army
5. Enable Action by Removing Barriers
6. Generate Short-Term Wins
7. Sustain Acceleration
8. Institute Change

To this day, Kotter's work is a major influence worldwide on organizations undergoing change. It is important to notice that all of the above steps have something to do with human interaction, rather than technical issues, which makes it an interesting playing field for people interested in psychology.

In 1997, Eliyahu M. Goldratt (1947-2011) invented *Critical Chain Project Management*. He based this on his earlier *Theory of Constraints*, which states that any manageable system is limited in achieving more of its goals by a small number of constraints, with there always being at least one constraint. Think of it as a more formal way of saying, "a chain is only as strong as its weakest link". Every time you've identified the weakest link and made it stronger, another link, or perhaps several links, become the weakest.

In his *Critical Chain Project Management* work, Goldratt poses that you should strive to keep resources leveled and require that they be flexible in start times. With resources he meant, people, equipment, and physical space. This differed from earlier methods, like the *Critical Path Method*, which emphasized task order and rigid scheduling. If resources are always available in unlimited quantities, then a project's *critical chain* is identical to its *critical path*, which, of course, is never the case. What is interesting about the *critical chain* idea, is that it introduces the idea of, "good is good enough". As far as can be known, there is no analytical method for finding an absolute optimum of the chain. The inherent uncertainty in estimates is much greater than the difference between the optimum and "good enough" solutions. This notion has had an effect on the way of thinking in organizations that cannot be underestimated. The collision between "operational excellence" and "good is good enough" has caused heated debates in many organizations.

In 2006, the Association for the Advancement of Cost Engineering, or AACE International, released its "Total Cost Management" framework, or TCM. Traditionally, the field of project management begins with the "initiation" of a project. However, it does not address what happens *before* a project is initiated. *Total Cost Management* maps the process upstream of project management. What precedes project management is referred to as "strategic asset management" or more traditionally, "portfolio and program management". TCM also addresses managing multiple projects as a *program* or *project portfolio*. TCM has found its widest audience in the companies that make large capital investments in fixed capital assets through construction projects, like oil and gas, chemical, pharmaceuticals, and utilities. However, the process is industry generic and found wider use in IT, software and other companies.

Even though *Agile* and its offspring have been around for two decades or more, traditional *project management* is still lurking around as well, much to the chagrin of *Agile* adepts. In as recently as 2012, the *ISO 21500:2012 Standard for Project Management* was released.

Technical background

In these last few paragraphs, there was a heavy focus on *project management*, which deals with the handling of a project, but not so much with the technical details of what is produced with the project. I find it important to touch on those aspects as well since some of the more technical paths of thinking accord with the project management way of thinking and are thus essential to understanding the psychology of today's work environment in most organizations, especially since the rise of the importance of *information technology* overall.

In 1979, Allan Albrecht of IBM introduced *Function Point* analysis. The *Function Point* is a unit of measurement to express the amount of business functionality an information system, as a product, provides to an end-user. Function points are used to compute a *Functional Size Measurement* of software. The costs, in money or hours, of a single unit, is based on experience from past projects. The functional user requirements of the software are identified and each one is categorized into different types. Once the function is identified and categorized into a type, it is then assessed for complexity and assigned a number of *Function Points*. The important thing to remember here is that this whole analysis is executed by very a small number of people involved in the setting up of the project at hand, and mostly based on a lot of assumptions since it is usually done *before* a project is actually undertaken. The *Function Point* analysis often serves as, at first, an aid for deciding on the viability of the project, and, later on, as a measuring rod for the progress of the project.

Similarly, a *Use Case Points* analysis can be used to calculate the estimated effort for a project, again, in money or hours. The *Use Case Points* technique was developed by Gustav Karner in 1993. The method is based on similar principles as the *Function Point* analysis but was designed specifically for so-called *object-oriented* systems and system requirements based on *Use Cases*. I mention this method in particular because it can still be found in practice and it often causes either rivalry or confusion with the *Agile* method of describing software functionality in so-called *User Stories*.

A *Use Case*, which is generally applied when the *Unified Modeling Language* (UML) and *Rational Unified Process* (RUP) methodologies are being used for software design and development, is a list of actions or event steps typically defining the interactions between an *actor* and a *system* to achieve a goal. The actor can be a human or other external system. This list results in detailed requirements that may even be considered as contractual statements. In short, a *Use Case* is extensive in the documentation and can, by definition, leave no light between what is needed by the business and what is to be delivered by the software developers.

In *User Stories*, however, a small piece of needed functionality is described with the use of a short format that looks like this:

As a [*type of user*],

I want [*short description of needed functionality*],

so I can [*result of working software being available*].

For instance:

As a *car driver*,

I want *my car to tell me how to drive to a certain given location*,

so I can *get in my car and drive without planning an itinerary*.

Notice that the *User Story* does not describe exactly what is to be programmed, it merely describes what the end result should be for the user. This leaves a lot of freedom, imagination, and negotiation room for the software developers to produce the solution. The psychological consequences of choosing either to work with *Use Cases* or *User Stories* are, not in the least for the software developers, as you might expect, enormous. Where the *Use Cases* describe every detail of what needs to be made, the *User Stories* leave a lot to the ingenuity of the software developers, and therefore also add to their responsibility.

Agile

I deliberately want to end this chapter with the *Agile Manifesto*. Not in the least because I wholeheartedly believe it to represent the right way of working in the twenty-first century.

Aptly, the *Agile Manifesto* was written at the very start of the twenty-first century, in 2001, by a small band of obscure techy smart-asses who were fed up with the then-current way of creating software, being traditional *project management*, with the stranglehold of the *iron triangle*, and with working in speed-obliterating vertical *silos* within large organizations.

These front-runners saw the limits to this way of working and its dire consequences if not acted upon. Moreover, they saw plenty of opportunities to cozy-up with the customers of their organizations, in order to succeed both tech-wise and business-wise.

Here is what the *Agile Manifesto* looks like:

Manifesto for Agile Software Development

We are uncovering better ways of developing

software by doing it and helping others do it.

Through this work we have come to value:

Individuals and interactions *over* processes and tools

Working software *over* comprehensive documentation

Customer collaboration *over* contract negotiation

Responding to change *over* following a plan

That is, while there is value in the items on

the right, we value the items on the left more.

It is not to be underestimated what these words have changed in the last few decades, in light of all that has been taught and lived by before the above mantra was introduced. Much of it squarely contradicts the traditional way of conducting *project management*.

We find even more oppositions towards traditional *project management* in the *twelve principles* behind the *Agile Manifesto*:

Our highest priority is to satisfy the customer

through early and continuous delivery

of valuable software.

Welcome changing requirements, even late in development. Agile processes harness change for the customer's competitive advantage.

Deliver working software frequently, from a couple of weeks to a couple of months, with a preference to the shorter timescale.

Business people and developers must work together daily throughout the project.

Build projects around motivated individuals. Give them the environment and support they need, and trust them to get the job done.

The most efficient and effective method of conveying information to and within a development team is face-to-face conversation.

Working software is the primary measure of progress.

Agile processes promote sustainable development.
The sponsors, developers, and users should be able
to maintain a constant pace indefinitely.

Continuous attention to technical excellence
and good design enhances agility.

Simplicity – the art of maximizing the amount
of work not done--is essential.

The best architectures, requirements, and designs
emerge from self-organizing teams.

At regular intervals, the team reflects on how
to become more effective, then tunes and adjusts
its behavior accordingly.

The Agile way of working completely negates the
careful planning upfront and then carrying out the
consecutive steps, within time, scope, and budget, to
complete the predefined project. Instead, Agile poses
that the best way to deal with the ever-faster changing
world, with its accompanying uncertainty, is to retrieve

feedback quickly and regularly on how things are going from all angles, for instance, from end-users and customers to your own team members, in order to adjust your work and, or, your way of working, to better suit the demands, and thus be more successful with each iteration.

The effect of the Agile movement on organizations worldwide cannot be understated. As writer Steve Denning (1944) puts it via his 2018 book title, we now live in "The Age of Agile". The subtitle of his book is, "How Smart Companies Are Transforming the Way Work Gets Done," which alludes in different ways to the attention organizations of today should be paying to this way of working. The *smart* part hints at the suggestion that if you don't work in an Agile way, you're selling yourself short. You might even say that in order to survive, organizations will *have* to turn to an Agile way of working. The last part, of *getting things done*, refers to the dogma within Agile that says things are only valuable to the end-user or customer if they're truly done. Agile practices a strict binary rule in this sense. The phrase that interests us most – from this book's point of view – is the *transforming* part, for that entails more than merely the *technical* transformations, which are numerous and grand in their own respect, but moreover, the *human* transformations of *thinking* and *attitude*.

From a psychological point of view, *Agile transformation* is as interesting as it is complex. Beyond the technical and organizational consequences, *Agile* has brought about changes in thinking about work motivation and satisfaction, and even the moral landscape, of the business world at large.

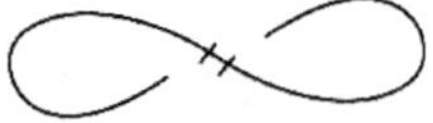

Epilogue – Proceed with Caution

You've learned a lot about psychology now and that has probably made you excited and eager to apply things in your workplace. I've also talked about the *Dunning-Kruger Effect* at the very start of this book. I caution you to be very aware of this effect.

The Peak of Mount Stupid

You have to realize that you might be on top of the *Peak of Mount Stupid*. Even though I'm very sure that the knowledge in this book is scientifically proven psychology, reading a book does not make you a psychologist, nor a psychotherapist. If you like what you've read, I encourage you to learn even more – you can follow online psychology courses from top universities like Yale, Cambridge, and many more. Start there, and who knows, maybe a bachelor's is next, or even a degree?

In the meantime, you can of course apply the knowledge you have gained from this book. It doesn't have the subtitle "*Practical* scientifically proven psychological insights into your mind and *everyday interactions with colleagues at work*" for nothing. Just be careful where you start. Don't start by conducting your very own *Stanford Prison Experiment* in the basement of your company. Please don't.

Where to Start after this Book

What you *can* do immediately – and I have no doubt you are already doing this – is to start to *recognize* certain psychological mechanisms at play during your everyday interactions at work. Once you start to recognize those and are able to recollect what they entail, you might be ready to throw in a little disruptive intervention – just to see if all plays out as you expected from what you've learned. After a number of these interventions, you will start to feel more comfortable in applying psychologically sound measures. Take it from there and learn as you go.

One thing I remember most from what I have learned about psychology is what I have described in the first chapter, in the segment about science in general. I said, "One thing that struck me about Professor Bloom's lectures, is the candor with which he proclaimed to be *uncertain* about a lot of things in the field of psychology." There is still so much left to be discovered, also by the people who are considered to be experts in the field. This tells me two things. For one, if you come across people who claim to know it all, don't trust them. And two, explore! Who's to say you are not the next person to figure out a very useful psychological model?

Good luck with your psychological endeavors!

Patrick Heller.

Appendix A – Timelines of Psychology, Work & History

Timelines

For completeness' sake, I've listed all the important stuff that I've described in chapter six and chapter seven, in two timelines, one for psychology, and one for work. Additionally, I've added a third timeline, which describes major political, technical, and otherwise interesting events, basically covering the same time period. These timelines should give you some context and background on when things evolved into the way they are today.

Psychology timeline

1637 René Descartes writes in his Discourse on the Method, "cogito, ergo sum"

1647 Thomas Hobbes releases Elementa Philosophica de Cive

1781 Immanuel Kant writes his Critique of Pure Reason

1859 Charles Darwin publishes his book On the Origin of Species

1879 Wilhelm Wundt opened the first psychology laboratory

1896 Sigmund Freud starts using psychoanalysis

1898 Edward Thorndike advances his Law of Effect

1901 Pavlov developed the concept of the conditioned reflex

1920 John B. Watson conducts classical conditioning experiments with Little Albert

1926 B.F. Skinner does experiments with Skinner Boxes

1934 Karl Popper puts forth his theory of potential falsifiability as the criterion separating science from non-science

1943 Abraham Maslow coins his Hierarchy of Needs

1949 ICD-6 (International Statistical Classification of Diseases and Related Health Problems) was published by the WHO (World Health Organization), the international standard diagnostic tool for epidemiology, health management, and clinical purposes, including a chapter about mental and behavioral disorders

1952 DSM-1 (Diagnostic and Statistical Manual of Mental Disorders) is released by the APA (American

Psychiatric Association), used for the classification of mental disorders

1957 Noam Chomsky releases Syntactic Structures

1963 Albert Bandura outlines his Social Learning Theory

1967 Ulric Neisser published Cognitive Psychology

1971 Neuroscience established as a discipline

1992 ICD-10 is released (most current version)

2013 DSM-5 is released (most current version)

2022 ICD-11 will be released, very much aligned on mental and behavioral disorders with DSM-5

Today Psychology is diverse: Abnormal, Biological, Cognitive, Developmental, Experimental, Evolutionary, Mathematical, Neuro, Personality, Psychophysics, and Social psychology

Work timeline

1600 British East India Company founded, multinational corporation

1602 Dutch East India Company founded, multinational corporation

1760 First Industrial Revolution, machine production methods, mass production

1870 Second Industrial Revolution, railroads, modern organizational methods

1896 Karol Adamiecki invents Harmonogram

1911 Frederick Winslow Taylor published his book The Principles of Scientific Management

1912 Henry Gantt invents Gantt Chart

1914 Lillian Moller Gilbreth writes her dissertation The Psychology of Management

1916 Henri Fayol publishes his article Administration industrielle et générale

1923 Max Weber's work is published as General Economic History

1926 Mary Parker Follett writes her essay The Giving of Orders

1924-1932 The Hawthorne Experiments

1954 Bernard Schriever coins the term project management

1954 Peter Drucker writes The Practice of Management in which he describes Management by objectives

1959 Peter Drucker coins the term knowledge worker

1960s Change management emerges

1962 Everett Rogers proposes the descriptions of Innovators, Early Adopters, Early Majority, Late Majority, and Laggards

1965 The IPMA, or International Project Management Association, was founded

1969 The PMI, the Project Management Institute, was founded

1970 Milton Friedman writes his article The Social Responsibility of Business is to Increase its Profits

1970 Winston Walker Royce describes the Waterfall Method

1977 The first project management software emerges

1979 Allan Albrecht of IBM introduces Function Point analysis

1982 W. Edwards Deming writes Quality, Productivity, and Competitive Position, including the *Plan-Do-Check-Act* cycle

1989 PRINCE was released, a structured project management method

1993 Daryl Conner coined the term *burning platform* in his book Managing at the Speed of Change
1993 Gustav Karner develops *Use Case* Points technique

1996 PRINCE2 was released, a generic project management method

1996 John P. Kotter releases his Leading Change

1997 Eliyahu M. Goldratt invented Critical Chain Project Management based on his earlier Theory of Constraints

2001 The Agile Manifesto is released, together with its twelve principles

2006 The Association for the Advancement of Cost Engineering releases its Total Cost Management framework

2012 The ISO releases its 21500:2012 Standard for Project Management

2017 Steve Denning writes his book The Age of Agile

Timeline of major political, technical, and otherwise interesting events

1440 Johannes Gutenberg invents the printing press

1568-1648 The Eighty Years' War or Dutch War of Independence (René Descartes lived in the Dutch Republic)

1776 American Declaration of Independence

1783 The Montgolfier brothers invent the hot air balloon

1789 French Revolution and the Declaration of the Rights of Man and of the Citizen

1800 Alessandro Volta invents the electrical circuit

1804 First steam locomotive hauled a train in South Wales

1826 Joseph Nicéphore Niépce takes the first photograph

1830s Samuel Morse and others invent the telegraph

1861-1865 American Civil War

1876 Alexander Graham Bell invents the telephone

1877 Thomas Edison invents the phonograph

1879 Thomas Edison invents the light bulb

1886 Karl Benz invents the automobile

1888 Nikola Tesla invents AC (*Alternating Current*) induction motor

1893 Count Ferdinand von Zeppelin invents the Zeppelin

1895 Guglielmo Marconi invents the radio

1895 Lumière brothers present the first film

1896 The first modern Olympics

1903 The Wright brothers fly the first airplane

1908 Henry Ford manufactures the Model T

1912 Titanic disaster

1914-1918 World War I

1917 The Russian Communist Revolution

1918-1920 The Spanish Flu

1927 Philo Taylor Farnsworth invents the television

1929 Wall Street Crash, followed by the Great Depression

1937 The Hindenburg disaster

1939-1945 World War II

After WWII *Das Wirtschaftswunder* in Germany and much of Northern Europe, as well as in Japan and (South-)Korea
1949 Mao establishes the *People's Republic of China*

1950-1953 Korean War

1955-1975 Vietnam War

1961 Yuri Gagarin is the first human in space

1963 US President Kennedy murdered

1969 Neil Armstrong sets foot on the Moon

1980s Soviet leader Mikhail Gorbachev introduces Perestroika and Glasnost (Restructuring and Openness)

1989 The fall of the Berlin Wall

1989 Tim Berners-Lee invents the World Wide Web

1990 German reunification

1991 Soviet Union dissolves

1991-1995 Yugoslav Wars

2001 9/11 terrorist attacks on the Twin Towers and the Pentagon, in the USA

2007-2008 Financial Crisis

2011-ongoing Syrian "Civil" War

2020 Coronavirus locks down much of Earth's human population for months on end, of which the consequences I cannot know when I'm writing this, since we're still in the middle of it as I type this, but it doesn't take a genius to foresee that this period will have its consequences in the fields of work, psychology, politics, and perhaps even our very way of life.

Some Things to Notice

To many of you, the above lists will no doubt read like utterly boring summations of historical events, where I see historical events unfold before my eyes. I see connections and I am truly amazed at how exciting some earlier eras were. We tend to think of our era, well into the twenty-first century, as a fast-paced time, filled with new inventions that make our world smaller and more connected. Today's world is often described as being a *VUCA-world – Volatile, Uncertain, Complex, and Ambiguous*. That might be true to some extent, but have a look at the nineteenth century, when railroads started to connect people physically, faster than ever before. People traveled across Europe, across America, across Asia. (Rich) people started to go on vacations in regions they never saw with their own eyes before, where people spoke different languages and had different customs, thus spreading their goods and knowledge and taking home other people's goods and knowledge.

Have a good look at the lists above and see that electricity, the train, the photograph, the telegraph, the telephone, the light bulb, the automobile, the electric motor, the radio, and film – and many more inventions I haven't listed – were all invented *before* 1900! For all these inventions – that still seem quite modern to us – that's at least more than 120 years ago...

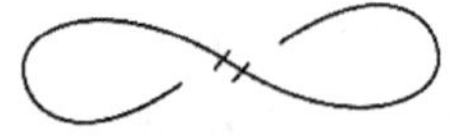

References

Note on the references: in this list below only those resources are included that are not specified fully in the main text. For instance, if the main text reads, "Neuroscientist Larry Cahill explains in his 2006 paper *Why sex matters for neuroscience* why we shouldn't be too politically correct about differences between sexes", then that paper is not mentioned below.

Preface   - Who should read this book and why?

If you're looking for a proper *Intro Psych* online, by sure to check out "Introduction to Psychology with Paul Bloom": https://www.youtube.com/playlist?list=PL6A08EB4EEFF3E91F

This course was recorded in Spring 2007. Complete course materials are available at the Yale Online website: online.yale.edu

Other fine online psychology courses include "Introduction to Psychology" from the University of Toronto, by Professor Steve Joordens: https://www.coursera.org/learn/introduction-psych/home/welcome

and "Social Psychology" from Wesleyan University, by Professor Scott Plous: https://www.coursera.org/learn/social-psychology/home/welcome

Especially this course has an enormous amount of resources available, including lots of reading material, but also a lot of video content.

Introduction - Your personal use of the book

University of Cambridge, Institute of Continuing Education (ICE): Applying psychology to the workplace: https://www.ice.cam.ac.uk/course/applying-psychology-workplace-1

Chapter One   - Beware the Nonsense

The Introduction to Psychology online course mentioned is this one on Coursera: https://www.coursera.org/learn/introduction-psychology/home/welcome

It is more or less the same as the Youtube video series from Yale with Paul Bloom that I've mentioned above (under Preface), but then in a more interactive Coursera format, with quizes, for instance.

"Unskilled and Unaware of It: How Difficulties in Recognizing One's Own Incompetence Lead to Inflated Self-Assessments" (1999) - in the Journal of Personality and Social Psychology - Justin Kruger and David Dunning.

"More the knowledge the lesser the ego, lesser the knowledge more the ego" - quote by Albert Einstein: https://www.quotes.net/quote/52742

"50 Great Myths of Popular Psychology" (2010) - Scott O. Lilienfeld, Steven Jay Lynn, John Ruscio, Barry L. Beyerstein.

"Great Myths of the Brain" (2015) - Christian Jarrett.

"10 Myths About the Mind" - Psychology Today magazine (October 2019) - Matt Huston.

"Mindset, The New Psychology of Success" (2006) - Carol S. Dweck.

"Neuro Linguistic Programming: Mental health veterans therapy fear" - https://www.bbc.com/news/uk-wales-24617644

"Tony Robbins talks about Robin Williams and fulfillment" - https://www.youtube.com/watch?v=BlVB9UPiphY

"Grief, And the Losses No One Talks About" - Psychology Today magazine (August 2020) - Hara Estroff Marano.

Chapter Two   - The Self

"Free Will" (2012) - Sam Harris.

"Thinking, Fast and Slow" (2011) - Daniel Kahneman.

Harvard University's "Project Implicit" - online research you can partake in to help the study into implicit biases - https://implicit.harvard.edu/implicit/takeatest.html

"Influence, The Psychology of Persuasion - Revised Edition" (2007) - Robert B. Cialdini.

"How to Inluence Others" - Robert Cialdini - https://www.youtube.com/watch?v=cILPoUtuDbQ

Chapter Three - The Self and Others

Asch's Conformity Experiment - https://www.youtube.com/watch?v=iRh5qy09nNw

Milgram's Obedience Experiment - https://www.youtube.com/watch?v=rdrKCilEhC0

"How monkeys mirror human irrationality" - Laurie Santos - https://www.youtube.com/watch?v=DUd8XA-5HEk

Chapter Four   - Therapy as Coaching

"Psychology", Eighth Edition (2018)- Peter Gray, David F. Bjorklund.

Chapter Five   - What's Next?

"Just Babies, The Origins of Good and Evil" (2013) - Paul Bloom.

"Against Empathy, The Case for Rational Compassion" (2016) - Paul Bloom.

"The Stanford Prison Experiment" (2017) - BBC Documentary - https://www.youtube.com/watch?v=F4txhN13y6A

Chapter Six   - The History of Psychology

"Psychology", Eighth Edition (2018)- Peter Gray, David F. Bjorklund.

Chapter Seven - The History of Work

"Leading Change" (1996) - John P. Kotter.

"The Age of Agile, How Smart Companies Are Transforming the Way Work Gets Done" (2018) - Stephen Denning.

Epilogue   - Proceed with Caution

"Unskilled and Unaware of It: How Difficulties in Recognizing One's Own Incompetence Lead to Inflated Self-Assessments" (1999) - in the Journal of Personality and Social Psychology - Justin Kruger and David Dunning.

Appendix A   - Timelines of Psychology, Work & History

https://en.wikipedia.org/wiki/Main_Page

https://en.wikipedia.org/wiki/Psychology

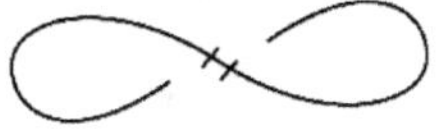

Index

10,000 hours of training, 40,
41
Aaron Beck, 192
ABC theory of emotions,
188, 189
Adrian Owen, 38
agile, 9, 10, 11, 45, 127, 139,
145, 157, 172, 188, 222,
245, 246, 250, 253, 255,
259, 261, 266, 267, 268
agilists, 9
Agile, ii, 61, 89, 110, 139,
147, 190, 201, 263, 264,
265, 266, 267, 278, 300
Agile Coach, 139, 190, 300
Agile Manifesto, 89, 263,
264, 278
Alan Baddeley, 91
Albert Bandura, 234, 275
social-cognitive theory,
234
Albert Einstein, 15, 20
Albert Ellis, 188, 192
Alfonse Caramazza, 37
Alfred D. Chandler, 241
Alzheimer, 27
Amos Tversky, 97, 169
amygdala, 25
Analogies, 93
Anatol Rapoport, 164

Aristotle, 220
Artificial Intelligence, 205
Astonishing Hypothesis, 69
attention, 6, 39, 59, 75, 79,
84, 88, 91, 113, 120, 159,
206, 266, 267
Attitudes, 127
authority figure, 148, 151
autism, 111
Autism, 27
autistic spectrum, 111
Autonomy, Mastery, and
Purpose, 153
availability bias, 98, 99
awareness, 7, 8, 91, 204,
210, 215, 242
Axelrod Tournaments, 164
axon, 32
axon terminals, 32
behavioral and cognitive
therapies, 185
behaviorism, 227, 229, 231,
232
Belbin, 178, 179, 180
team roles, 178
Bernard Schriever, 249, 276
biases, vii, 8, 54, 97, 102,
103, 106, 134, 210, 213,
215, 235, 248
Biases, 97, 169

attractiveness bias, 114
Availability Bias, 98, 101
Confirmation Bias, 99,
    101
Predictable-World Bias,
    102, 103
Big Five, 73, 74
Binet-Simon, 75
    Alfred Binet, 74
    David Wechsler, 75
    Stanford-Binet Scale, 75
    Théodore Simon, 74
    WAIS-IV, 76
Bloom, 13, 15, 211, 270
brainpower, 19, 20
Brain-training, 37
Brooke Macnamara, 41
Buddha, 220
bureaucracy, 243, 245
Bystander Effect, 156
    Kitty Genovese, 157
Carl Jung, 50
Carl Rogers, 183, 232, 233
Carl-Gustav Jung, 225
Carol Dweck, 45, 46, 47, 48,
    49, 50
Change Management, 251
Charles Darwin, 223, 274
Charles Hume, 39
Charles Spearman, 78
Choking under pressure, 138
chunks of memory, 85
classical conditioning, 186,
    228, 229, 274
    conditioned stimulus, 228

neutral response, 228
neutral stimulus, 228
unconditioned response,
    228
unconditioned stimulus,
    228
Claude Steele, 140
client-centered therapy, 183
climate change, 16
Cognitive Behavioral
    Therapy, 185
cognitive bias, 12, 248
cognitive biases, 98
Cognitive Dissonance, 129
Cognitive Therapy, 188
command-and-control, 153
common stereotype, 134
communication skill level,
    199
company culture, 154
confederates, 145
confirmation bias, 99, 101
Conformity, 143
Confucius, 220
consciousness, 91, 93, 231
Contingency management,
    186
cooperative self-
    organization, 153
corpus callosum, 21, 23
Daniel Kahneman, 90, 97,
    169
Daryl Conner, 256, 277
David Chalmers, 91

decision making, 25, 29, 31,
127, 129, 131, 211, 214
Deduction, 104
definition of psychology,
219
Demand Effect, 120
dendrites, 32
direct hierarchy, 243
DISC, 51, 52, 53, 54, 178,
180
Donald Cardwell, 239
Cardwell's Law, 239
Douglas McGregor, 147
DSM-5, 275
dualistic view, 69, 221
Dunning-Kruger Effect, 12,
269
Peak of Mount Stupid,
13, 14, 269
valley of despair, 12
East India Companies, 240
eclectic, 195
Edward Thorndike, 229, 274
puzzle boxes for cats, 229
Eliyahu M. Goldratt, 257,
277
Theory of Constraints,
257, 277
Elton Mayo, 120
Emotional Intelligence, 77
emotional responses, 25
empathy, 35, 37, 210, 211,
213, 214
Empathy, 210, 211

empiricism, 222, 223
encoding, 84, 86, 88, 89
Enron, 46, 47
Everett Rogers, 251, 276
Executive Functions, 79, 82,
84
inhibition, 79, 82, 84
switching, 79, 82, 84
working memory, 38, 39,
79, 83, 84, 86, 88, 91,
92, 138
explicit and implicit
attitudes, 127, 128, 134
explicit attitudes, 127, 129,
130
Fake News, 14
post-truth, 14
far transfer, 39
Fibonacci sequence, 146
fight, flight, or *freeze* model,
29
Five Dysfunctions of a
Team, 124, 176
fixed-ratio schedule, 231
fMRI, 20, 23, 26, 33, 34, 95
Francis Crick, 69
Frans de Waal, 166
Frans De Waal, 204
Frederic Laloux, 128
Frederick Winslow Taylor,
242, 276
Taylorism, 242
free association, 225
Free Will, 70

Freud, 51, 182, 183, 195, 224, 225, 226, 227, 274
Fritz Heider, 113
functional fixedness, 107
fundamental attribution error, 113, 114, 125
game theory, 164, 165
games, 37, 38, 40, 41, 168
George A. Miller, 85
George Odiorne, 250
Giacomo Rizzolatti, 35
global warming, 18
goal setting, 198
Google Walkouts, 202
Gordon Allport, 72, 127
Gray and Bjorklund, 219, 220
grief, 67, 251
group dynamics, 178
growth mindset, 45, 46, 47, 48, 49, 50, 63
    fixed mindset, 45, 46, 48
    talent mindset, 46
habituation, 188
hard problem, 91
Hawthorne, 11, 119, 120, 247, 248, 276
Hawthorne experiments, 11, 120
hemispheres of the brain, 11, 12
Henri Fayol, 242, 276
    Fayolism, 242
Henry A. Landsberger, 120, 248
Henry Gantt, 242, 276
    Gantt Chart, 242, 276
heritability
    heritability coefficient, 80
Heritability, 80
Heuristics, 97, 169
hierarchy of needs, 233
high-performance, 124, 198
High-Performance team, 177
high-performance teams, 124
hippocampus, 25, 30, 89
Honey & Mumford's model, 43
human resources, 10
Humanistic psychotherapy, 183
humanists, 234
hyperconnectivity, 115
Id, the Ego and the Super-ego, 225
Immanuel Kant, 223, 273
    a posteriori knowledge, 223
    a priori knowledge, 223
implicit attitudes, 128, 134
implicit stereotype, 134, 135
Impression Management, 141
    conscious impression management, 142
incubation period, 107

Influence by Example, 142
    informational influence, 143
    normative influence, 143
in-groups and out-groups, 213
In-groups and Out-groups, 131
Insight Problems, 106
insufficient-justification effect, 131
intelligence, 37, 38, 40, 41, 45, 47, 63, 74, 77, 78, 79, 80, 81, 82, 83, 84, 93, 94, 101, 105
    crystallized intelligence, 37, 78, 82
    fluid intelligence, 37, 38, 78, 82
    g as the general underlying factor of intelligence, 78
interpersonal relations, 109
IQ tests, 75, 76, 82, 94
irrational behavior, 170
Ivan Pavlov, 227
Jacob Cohen, 26
    Cohen's d, 26, 27
Jane Goodall, 214
John Gray, 24
    Men are from Mars, Women are from Venus, 24
John Grinder, 55
John P. Kotter, 256, 277

John von Neumann, 165
Karl Anders Ericsson, 40
Karl Marx, 225
Karl Popper, 226, 274
Karol Adamiecki, 242, 276
    Harmonogram, 242, 276
language, 22, 23, 24, 30, 34, 56, 92, 96, 234
Larry Cahill, 27
Laurie Santos, 168
Learning, 88, 90, 275
Lee Ross, 113
Lencioni, 124, 178
Lenore Jacobson, 118
Leon Festinger, 129
Leonardo Fogassi, 35
Lillian Moller Gilbreth, 246, 276
limbic system, 28, 29
Little Albert, 229, 274
lizard brain, 11, 28, 29, 30, 31
loss aversion, 169, 170, 171, 172, 173
Loss Aversion, 168
Luigi Galvani, 33
Magical Number Seven, 85
Malcolm Gladwell, 40, 232
    10,000 hours rule, 232
male and female brain differences, 25
map is not the territory, 56
Mark Leary, 121

marketing, 21, 155
Martin Seligman, 196
Martin Theodore Orne, 120
Mary Parker Follett, 245,
    250, 276
Maslow, 147, 232, 233, 274
materialism, 221
Matthias Mehl, 26
Max Weber, 243, 276
McKinsey, 46
meaning of dreams, 225
measurable goals, 198
memory, 18, 25, 30, 31, 37,
    38, 39, 41, 63, 75, 76, 78,
    79, 82, 83, 84, 86, 87, 88,
    89, 91, 92, 94, 105, 138,
    139
    central executive, 91
    episodic buffer, 92
    phonological loop, 91, 92
    short-term memory, 84,
        92
    visuospatial sketchpad,
        91
Memory, 83, 87
metrics, 185, 198, 199
Michael Gazzaniga, 21
Michael Vendetti, 96
Miller's law, 85
Milton Friedman, 252, 277
mindfulness, 195
mirror neurons, 11, 35, 36
    broken mirror neurons,
        36
    broken mirror system, 36

Monica Melby-Lervåg, 39
mood baseline, 67
moral compass, 201
moral sense, 206
Morality, 201, 202, 203,
    204, 205, 206, 207, 211,
    233
Morton Ann Gernsbacher,
    36
Motivational coaches, 66
Myer-Briggs Type Indicator,
    51, 54, 178, 180
Myers-Briggs Type
    Indicator, 50
nativism, 223
nature versus nurture, 80
near transfer, 39
neocortex, 28, 30
Net Promoter Score, 199
neurons, 20, 32, 33, 35, 36
neuroscience, 20, 27, 30, 31,
    33, 34, 36
Neuroscience, 235, 275
NLP, 55, 56, 57, 58, 59, 60,
    61, 62, 65, 66, 67
Noam Chomsky, 234, 275
Nobel Prize, 21, 69, 97, 169
nucleus, 32
Obedience, 148, 150
observational learning, 234
observer-expectancy effect,
    248
OCEAN, 73

Agreeableness, 74
Conscientiousness, 53, 73
Extraversion, 73
Neuroticism, 74
Openness, 73, 280
Oedipus complex, 225
operant conditioning, 230, 231
Organizational psychology, 2
Oskar Morgenstern, 165
outcome metric, 199
pandemic, 18
PAPI, 54
partial reinforcement, 231
Patrick Lencioni, 124, 176
Paul Bloom, 11, 204, 211, 214
Paul Broca, 34
Broca's area, 34
Paul D. MacLean, 28
penis-envy, 225
performance metric, 199
personal identity, 132
Personality, 50, 71, 236, 275
Personality tests, 50
person-based therapy, 183
person-centered approach, 233
persuasion, 155
Peter Drucker, 249, 276
Peter Wason, 100
Philip Zimbardo, 216
Phillipa Foot, 207
physical healthcare, 196
Plan-Do-Check-Act cycle, 255, 277
Plan-Do-Study-Act cycle, 255
Plato, 220
point of no return, 130
Poker Planning, 145
polygraph, 51
positive illusory bias, 125
Positive Psychology, 196, 197
Post-Traumatic Stress Disorder, 64
preferred learning style, 42, 43, 44
prefrontal cortex, 95
prejudice, vii, 132, 136, 210, 213, 233
presuppositions, 56, 61
PRINCE2, 254, 277
Prisoner's Dilemma, 163, 164, 165
Prisoner's Dilemma, 162
private explicit stereotype, 134, 135
process metrics, 199
Project Management, 249, 252, 257, 258, 259, 277, 278
prospect theory, 97, 169
pseudoscience, 54, 62, 226
Pseudoscience, 51

psychoanalyst, 183
psychodynamic, 182, 184,
    185, 188, 190, 192, 195,
    225
psychodynamic
    psychotherapy, 182, 190,
    225
psychological freedom, 239
psychotherapists, 62, 181
public explicit stereotype,
    134, 135
Pygmalion Effect, 117, 118,
    119, 120, 121
racism, 99, 101
Rapport, 57
rational compassion, 214
Raven's Progressive
    Matrices test, 94
Raymond Cattell, 72, 78
reasoning
    inductive reasoning, 97,
        103, 105
Reasoning, 93, 96, 105
Reference Groups, 122
    social comparison, 122
Reinventing Organizations,
    128
reliability, 17, 51
René Descartes
    Cogito ergo sum, 221
René Descartes, 69, 221
René Descartes, 240
René Descartes, 273
René Descartes, 278

repressed, 225
reptilian complex, 28, 30
retrieval, 84, 87, 89, 90
Richard Bandler, 55
Rita Carter, 36
Robert Cialdini, 155
Robert Rosenthal, 118
Robert Zajonc, 137
Roger Sperry, 21
Rosalie Rayner, 229
rules of thumb, 97
running therapy, 195
Sally and Anne test, 111
Sam Harris, 70
science, 2, 3, 4, 8, 15, 51, 68,
    109, 166, 219, 220, 226,
    235, 270, 274
Scientific management, 242,
    245
Scrum, 85, 124, 139, 157,
    164, 188, 222, 255, 300
Scrum Master, 124, 139,
    157, 300
Scrum Sprints, 164
Self-actualization, 232
Self-esteem, 121
self-fulfilling prophecy, 118,
    140
Self-serving Attributional
    Bias, 125
self-talk, 198
senses, 59, 83, 84, 222
sensory experiences, 222

sensory memory, 84

skill balance, 199

Skinner, 229, 230, 231, 234, 274

   Skinner boxes, 229, 230

social facilitation, 137

social identity, 132

social interference, 136, 137, 138

social media, 1, 14, 17, 68, 117, 176, 196, 210

Social Norms, 154

social pressure, 136, 137, 139, 141, 142

Social Pressure, 136

social psychology, 109, 113, 129, 162, 217

sociology, 243

sociometer theory, 121, 122

Socrates, 220

Socratic Questioning, 192, 194

   Powerful questions, 192

Solomon Asch, 143

soma, 32

Sport Psychology, 198

sports, 41, 105, 106, 114, 123, 125, 131, 138, 198, 232

Stanford Prison Experiment, 216, 270

Stanley Milgram, 148

stereotype threat, 140

stereotypes, vii, 132, 134, 135, 136, 141, 210, 213

stretched goals, 172, 173

Stuckness, 58

Susanne Jaeggi, 38

system one thinking, 98

tabula rasa, 234

Teal organization, 128

team happiness, 199

team performance, 124

tests with twins, 81

The Surprising Truth About What Motivates Us, 153

Theory of Evolution, 223

Theory of Mind, 110, 112

Theory X & Y, 147, 148

Therapist, 181

therapists, 55, 56, 66, 175, 182, 183, 187, 192, 195, 226, 235

therapy, 6, 58, 181, 182, 184, 185, 186, 187, 188, 190, 192, 193, 195, 196, 227

Therapy, xi, 175, 186, 195, 286

think outside the box, 107

Thinking Fast and Slow, 90

   system one thinking, 90

   system two thinking, 90, 215

Thomas Hobbes, 221, 273

Tit-for-tat, 164

Tony Robbins, 65

Torkel Klingsberg, 38

toxic positivity, 126, 197

Toxic positivity, 67

Traits, 71, 72

transformation, 10, 11, 102, 156, 257, 268

tribes, 109

Triune Brain, 28

Trolley Problem, 207

Tuckman, 176
    Forming, Storming, Norming, and Performing, 176
    Stages of Group Development, 176

Ultimatum Game, 165, 204

unethical experiments, 229

validity, 51, 54, 75

values, 127, 217

variable-ratio schedule, 231

victim-blaming, 66

Vilayanur Ramachandran, 35

visualization, 89, 198

visuospatial processing, 39

VUCA-world, 281

W. Edwards Deming, 254, 277

Walter Clarke, 53

Walter Shewhart, 255

Watson, 229, 274

WEIRD, 215, 216

Wilhelm Wundt, 78, 220, 224, 226, 274

William James, 19

William Moulton Marston, 51, 52, 53

Winston Walker Royce, 253, 277

workplace, 3, 10

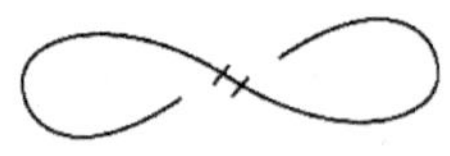

About the author

Patrick Heller has experienced many organizations on the inside as a coach and consultant. His career path has taken him from being a software developer in the nineties to a Scrum Master in the zeros to an Agile Coach in the last decade. He has successfully helped organizations to become more responsive and Agile in order for them to succeed in today's fast-changing circumstances.

Patrick's special interests go out to Leadership and Psychology. He found the psychological aspects of coaching more and more intriguing, and that was the reason for expanding his knowledge in these areas with great passion in the last several years. Now he deems the time ripe to share some of that wisdom with people who work at modern organizations and find themselves contemplating how helpful it would be to know more about the inner workings of the human mind and the way it interacts with others.

You can contact the author via e-mail at patrick@psychologyforwork.com or visit his website at https://psychologyforwork.com

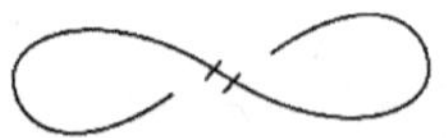